IMPROVING PARENTAL INVOLVEMENT

Related titles from Cassell:

David Collins: *Managing Truancy in Schools*

Linda Evans: *Managing to Motivate*

Anne Gold: *Head of Department: Principles in Practice*

Keith Topping: *Paired Reading, Writing and Spelling: The Handbook for Teachers and Parents*

Sheila Wolfendale and Keith Topping: *Family Involvement in Literacy: Effective Partnerships in Education*

Improving Parental Involvement

Garry Hornby

CASSELL
London and New York

Cassell

Wellington House
125 Strand
London WC2R 0BB

370 Lexington Avenue
New York
NY 10017–6550

First published 2000

British Library Cataloguing-in-Publication Data
A catalogue record for this book is available from the British Library.

ISBN 0-304-70551-9 (hardback)
      0-304-70552-7 (paperback)

Typeset by Kenneth Burnley, Wirral, Cheshire.
Printed and bound in Great Britain by Biddles Ltd, Guildford and King's Lynn.

Contents

For

Richard and Adam,

*who have enabled me to add a parent's perspective
to that of a teacher*

Introduction

After working with parents as a mainstream and special class teacher, educational psychologist, researcher and teacher educator, as well as being a parent of two young children, I have come to believe that a collaborative working relationship between teachers and parents is a key factor in providing the optimum education for children. I now consider that developing the interpersonal skills, attitudes and knowledge needed for working effectively with parents is essential for all teachers.

My first experience of the benefits of teachers working closely with parents happened when I was 10 years of age. Around the age of 7 I had developed a stammer which had got progressively worse. My parents had consulted the family doctor who made a referral to a speech therapist. I went to speech therapy for about half a dozen sessions but it didn't seem to help. By the time I was in my final year at primary school my parents were very concerned about the problem but were at a loss about what else to try. Then, at a parents' evening, my teacher suggested that elocution lessons would help and gave my parents the name of someone she recommended. As you can appreciate, as we lived in a working-class area of Rochdale, elocution lessons were not something which parents automatically considered for their children! Nevertheless, I started attending once a week and almost immediately the fluency of my speech improved. After a year my stammer was hardly noticeable and, in fact, I passed the grade one elocution examination with distinction! Though I stopped attending elocution after this, my stammer has remained under reasonable control ever since. I can still find certain words difficult to start sentences with and sometimes feel uncomfortable using the telephone, but I am now only aware of working hard to control my stammer when I get nervous in situations such as lecturing to very large groups of people.

The help my teacher gave to my parents has had a significant impact on my life. I would never have been able to work as a teacher, educational psychologist or university lecturer if I had not learned to control my stammer when I did: not to mention the potentially devastating effect on my personal life which this difficulty with oral communication could have led to. So I am acutely aware of the debt I owe to this teacher, who had the interests of her pupils at heart and who used her knowledge of how my special need could be met and her interpersonal skills to persuade my parents to try something they would not have thought of themselves.

My professional interest in the benefits of teachers working closely with parents emerged when I was teaching adolescents with moderate learning difficulties in a secondary school special class in New Zealand 25 years ago. Several incidents which occurred at that time highlighted the importance of having good working relationships with parents and stimulated my interest in learning more about this aspect of the teacher's role. Some of the experiences I had with parents are documented in Chapter 6. These experiences gave me the incentive to learn more about working with parents.

Over the past 25 years I have developed this interest and have conducted numerous workshops with parents. In recent years I have specialized in providing in-service training for teachers on working with parents. In this book I have drawn on these experiences in order to provide information which will help teachers develop the attitudes, knowledge and skills considered essential for working effectively with parents.

This book is intended to provide teachers with guidelines for improving parental involvement in their schools in order to facilitate the healthy development of all children, including those who have special needs of any kind.

The first chapter provides a rationale for establishing effective working relationships with parents and outlines the attitudes, skills and knowledge which teachers need to develop. Factors which influence levels of parental involvement and typical ways in which parents are involved with schools are also discussed. Chapter 2 discusses various approaches to working with parents and presents a model to guide the practice of parental involvement which addresses parents' needs and also their strengths. A checklist of aspects of parent involvement which need to be addressed in designing policy and procedures for working with parents is considered. Chapter 3 discusses various methods for improving communication with parents, such as making home visits, improving parent–teacher meetings and using different forms of written communication. Chapter 4 considers the various forms of parental involvement in children's education. This includes parental involvement in assessments and reviews of progress, home–school reading programmes and home–school behaviour programmes. Chapter 5 outlines the interpersonal skills needed by teachers in order to work effectively with parents. These include listening skills, counselling skills and assertion skills. Chapter 6 focuses on working with parents in groups such as in parent education programmes or workshops. The organizational and group leadership skills needed by teachers in order to work with groups of parents are also discussed. Chapter 7 addresses the needs of parents of children with disabilities and those with health problems. It considers the process which parents and other family members go through in adapting to a child's disability or medical condition. Also discussed is how parents and their children are affected by the environment in which they live. Chapter 8 addresses the needs of parents of children who have experienced a loss through bereavement or divorce. Chapter 9 addresses the challenge of working with parents who present special difficulties to teachers. Finally, Chapter 10 discusses overall strategies for improving parental involvement in schools.

Acknowledgements

I would like to thank all the parents, teachers and other colleagues, too numerous to mention, with whom I have worked over the years, many of whom have contributed to the ideas presented in this book.

Chapter 1

Rationale for Improving Parental Involvement

> Parents are critical to children's successes during the school years.
> (Ballantine, 1999, p. 170)

A frequent complaint of teachers is that the parents they most want to see seldom come into schools (Karther and Lowden, 1997). This view is borne out by the typically low levels of parental involvement in schools in deprived areas and those which take in a large proportion of children with special needs. In fact, minimal parental involvement in schools is an international phenomenon, with the majority of parents worldwide having little contact with the schools which their children attend (Epstein, 1990).

The aim of this book is to provide some guidelines for changing this situation; that is, for increasing the participation of a greater proportion of parents in the education of their children. Increased parental involvement is important because of the benefits that parental involvement brings. Sussell *et al.* (1996) suggest that these include:

- more positive parental attitudes toward teachers and schools;
- more positive student attitudes and behaviours;
- improved student performance;
- improved teacher morale;
- improved school climate.

The list of potential benefits is extended by Karther and Lowden (1997) who consider that the major benefits of parental involvement include:

- student gains in various areas;
- increased parental satisfaction with schools;
- increased self-confidence of parents involved;
- overall school improvement.

In addition, Ballantine (1999) suggests that the positive outcomes of parental involvement also include:

- improved communication between parents and children;
- higher academic performance of the children whose parents are involved;
- high school attendance and less disruptive behaviour;
- increased likelihood of completing high school and attending college;
- a sense of accomplishment for parents;
- higher parental expectations of children;
- improved study habits among children;
- increased likelihood of parents deciding to continue their own education.

The importance of parental involvement is reinforced by the considerable amount of research evidence which is now available to support the contention that improving parental involvement increases the effectiveness of the education that children receive. Reviews of the literature consistently provide support for the effectiveness of parental involvement in facilitating children's development. Reviews of numerous studies of the links between parent involvement and children's achievement have concluded that the evidence that parent involvement improves student achievement is beyond dispute (Henderson, 1987; Henderson and Berla, 1994).

Swap (1993) reports that these gains are made when parents are simply involved as supporters of their children's learning or are just kept informed about their progress at school. However, she states that the greatest gains are made when parents are more directly involved, such as when they act as tutors with their children. She gives examples of successful projects at pre-school, primary and secondary levels for which parent involvement was a major component. These are outlined below.

At the pre-school level Swap cites the Perry Preschool Project in the USA (Berrueta-Clement *et al.*, 1984) which included 1½-hour weekly home visits for all children in the project and their mothers. Children who participated in the programme had significantly higher IQs than control group children throughout their first two years at school. Although IQ differences disappeared after this, a follow-up study revealed that the programme produced important long-term benefits. These included increased academic achievement, decreased need for special education placement, less unemployment and fewer contacts with the criminal justice system. It has been suggested that involving parents was the key to maintaining the benefits of the programme.

At the primary school level Swap cites a British study (Tizard *et al.*, 1982) which compared the effects of parental involvement in their children's reading with the provision of additional specialist tutorial assistance with reading at school. The results showed that primary school children who read aloud to their parents two to four times a week from books sent home from school made significantly greater gains in reading achievement than children receiving additional assistance at school!

Studies of parental involvement at the secondary school level are scarcer than those of primary or pre-school programmes. Swap cites a study of parent involvement in mathematics in which she was one of the researchers (Moses *et al.*, 1989). This project relied heavily on parent involvement in order to improve the achievement of secondary school pupils in mathematics. Parents were involved in several ways: as project leader; through informational meetings; through participation in workshops; and by acting as voluntary classroom helpers. The project produced a substantial improvement in mathematics performance for the students involved compared with the achievement of previous years of students. This result was attributed mainly to the high level of parental involvement in the project.

It is clear from the above examples that involving parents promotes children's achievement from pre-school through secondary education. Therefore, establishing and maintaining high levels of parental involvement in schools is an essential element in ensuring their effectiveness in providing the best possible education for the children they serve. However, the extent to which this can be achieved is influenced by the presence of certain barriers to parental involvement.

BARRIERS TO PARENTAL INVOLVEMENT

I have lived and worked for a number of years in three very different countries: England, New Zealand, and Barbados. Analysing the strengths and weaknesses of parental involvement in each of these countries has led me to conclude that there is a set of factors which influence the levels and types of parental involvement in schools which exist in each of the countries. These influential factors are discussed below.

Demographic changes

There have been two major changes in families in the last few decades which have made parental involvement in schools more difficult. First, a majority of mothers of school-aged children are now in the workforce. Second, since in many countries almost half of all marriages end in divorce, a substantial proportion of children live in single-parent families. In fact, in Barbados, single-parent families headed by mothers are so prevalent they are considered the norm! When both parents are working or there is only one parent in the home it is much more difficult for these parents to have high levels of involvement in their children's education.

Historical/societal factors

In some societies, such as in Barbados, there is no history or societal expectation of parental involvement in schools or even in the education of their children. Schools are seen as places where children are sent to be educated. Parents are not expected to be involved in schools or even in educating their

children at home. Educating children is seen as the job of teachers and this is
to occur in schools! While these views are gradually changing in modern-day
Barbados, they remain much more ingrained than in other countries such as
New Zealand, which makes it very difficult to establish satisfactory levels of
parent involvement there.

Policy/legislation on parental involvement

In countries where there is legislation and agreed policy on parental involvement such as in the USA and England, it is much easier to maintain high levels
of parent involvement than in countries where these are not in place, such as
in Barbados.

Parent attitudes

Epstein (1990) from her numerous studies of parental involvement concludes
that almost all parents from all backgrounds care about the education of their
children. So it is not a lack of interest on behalf of parents which leads to low
levels of parental involvement. Epstein suggests that it is the fact that so few of
them know what schools expect from them or how they might contribute to
their child's schooling which is at the core of the problem. It is this lack of
knowledge which acts as a barrier to the establishment of high levels of
parental involvement.

Organization of school system

It is much easier to establish high levels of parental involvement in countries
like New Zealand where nearly all children walk to their local schools than in
places like Barbados where many children are transported to schools outside
the area in which they live. Where children attend their local schools it is easier
to get parents involved with the schools which they see as a part of their communities; whereas, because an 11-plus exam system is still in place in Barbados
to determine secondary school placement, parents transport their children to
what they consider are the best primary schools, wherever they are on the
island. Also, secondary school students criss-cross the island in order to get to
the schools for which they won entry. This system leads to a situation in which
schools are not identified with their local communities, and this makes it difficult to ensure satisfactory levels of parental involvement.

School culture

The more autocratic the management structure of schools, the less likely they
are to be able to sustain parental involvement which is based on partnerships
between parents and teachers. Where collaboration is not the norm among
staff at the school it is unlikely that the collaboration between parents and
teachers which is necessary for effective parental involvement will be possible.

Since autocratic styles of management are the norm in many countries, this is another factor which contributes to low levels of parental involvement.

School policy and procedures

In order for schools to effectively involve parents, they must have clear policies and well-established procedures for working with parents. School policies are influenced by national and regional policies but also vary from school to school depending on the views of teachers and in particular head-teachers and boards of governors. Some schools do not have an overt or even a consistent covert policy on parental involvement, and this is then another barrier.

Resources

Increasing levels of parental involvement involve increasing amounts of teachers' time. Where teachers are already stretched because of poor working conditions or lack of resources, or because a disproportionate amount of their time is spent on paperwork, it is difficult to convince them that they need to contribute more time if they are to set up effective schemes of parental involvement. Additional financial and human resources need to be provided in order to facilitate high levels of parental involvement, but these are very hard to come by these days. A few years ago some English schools, particularly in deprived areas, were provided with home–school liaison teachers who taught half time and used their remaining time for parental involvement. This worked extremely well but has now just about died out due to lack of funding.

Teacher training

As Epstein (1985) points out, the majority of teachers have had little or no training on working with parents on either initial training courses or as a part of in-service training. Most teachers, therefore, lack the skills and knowledge needed for effectively working with parents, and this is another barrier to setting up high levels of parent involvement.

Teacher attitudes

Positive teacher attitudes to working with parents are clearly essential if parental involvement is to be successful. However, many teachers have negative attitudes towards collaborating with parents, as is elaborated below.

ATTITUDES OF TEACHERS TOWARDS PARENTS

Research conducted with teachers indicates that they find interactions with parents to be a major source of stress in their jobs (Turnbull and Turnbull, 1986). Parents too are reported to find communications with teachers to be equally stressful. In fact, Sonnenschien (1984) has suggested that certain common attitudes which many teachers hold towards parents can contribute substantially towards this stress. These include the fact that parents are often viewed as being either problems or adversaries. Alternatively, they are seen as vulnerable, less able or in need of treatment themselves. In addition, parents are sometimes considered to be the cause of their children's problems. Finally, for various reasons, perhaps related to the above views, many professionals adopt an attitude of 'professional distance'. These common attitudes towards parents are discussed below, followed by discussion of attitudes which are more conducive to the development of effective working partnerships with parents.

Parents as problems

Some teachers see parents mainly as problems. When parents are convinced there is something wrong with their child despite reassurance from professionals, they are considered to be 'over-anxious'. When parents disagree with a diagnosis or the results of an assessment and ask for a second opinion they are said to be 'denying the reality' of the situation. When parents refuse to accept the educational programmes or placements suggested for their child, and are adamant about what they want, they are regarded as being 'aggressive'. Labelling parents in these ways makes it more difficult to develop productive working relationships with them.

Parents as adversaries

There is a tendency for teachers to view parents as adversaries. Teachers may have different goals and priorities to parents concerning the educational programmes of the children that they teach. This can create conflict and sometimes competition between parents and teachers. Competition can also be focused on children's achievements. Typically, children will behave more appropriately for their teachers than they will for their parents. In contrast, parents often report that children do things at home which are not observed at school. In these situations it is easy for either teachers or parents to feel doubtful or resentful about the others' success in getting the child to perform well. Avoiding the tendency to view parents as adversaries is essential for good relationships.

Parents as vulnerable

Teachers may regard parents as being too vulnerable to be treated as equal partners. This occurs most often when teachers are reluctant to tell parents the whole truth about their child's difficulties in case they become upset. So some of the child's weaknesses may be glossed over or parents may be given an overly optimistic view of their child's likely future progress. This does not promote the development of good relationships, since parents are widely reported to appreciate teachers telling them all that they know about the child's difficulties as honestly as possible (see Chapter 7).

Alternatively, teachers who come across as 'superior' will actually contribute to feelings of vulnerability in parents, which may lead to them becoming defensive and resistant to suggestions. Feeling vulnerable is an understandable reaction in parents who are seeking help for their child. Therefore, teachers should strive to allay this feeling, not add to it, as they sometimes unintentionally do, by developing the skills necessary for communicating sensitively and effectively with parents (as described in Chapter 5).

Parents as less able

There is a tendency for parents to be viewed as less observant, less perceptive and less intelligent than teachers. Therefore, parents' ideas and opinions are not given the credence which they deserve. This is a pity since most parents have an abundance of information about their children which can be invaluable to their teachers. A more helpful view is to consider that, while teachers are the experts on education, parents are the experts on their own children.

Parents as needing treatment

Some teachers believe that many parents who have children with problems find this difficult to accept and therefore are in need of counselling. This assumed weakness in parents then becomes the focus of attention rather than the child. Such views are experienced as patronizing and extremely frustrating by parents. It is therefore unwise to make assumptions about possible difficulties which parents may have. It is generally more helpful for the development of productive relationships when teachers focus on parents' strengths rather than their weaknesses.

Parents as causal

Another possible attitudinal barrier to developing effective working relationships with parents occurs when teachers consider that parents have caused or contributed to children's problems. This tends to happen more with children who have emotional or behavioural difficulties. These are often considered by teachers to be caused by parents who have deprived their children of love or discipline. But even with children who have learning difficulties, there is a tendency to assume that these have been made worse by poor parenting.

Many parents who have children with difficulties experience guilt for one reason or another. Some wonder whether they are in any way responsible for causing the problems, while others feel guilty about not being able to spend more time working with their children in order to overcome their difficulties. Therefore, it is of no benefit for teachers to add to these guilt feelings by communicating to parents either indirectly or directly their views about the parents' role in causing their children's problems.

Parents needing to be kept at a 'professional distance'

Many teachers prefer to keep parents at a professional distance: they don't want to establish close working relationships with parents in case this causes problems. This attitude can result from teachers subscribing to any of the negative attitudes discussed above or can be due to a lack of confidence about being able to relate well to parents. Also, the necessity for emotional distance to be maintained between professionals and their clients is an attitude which in the past has been encouraged on many professional training courses. Unfortunately, parents perceive this emotional distance as being indicative of the lack of empathy teachers have with their situation. They therefore typically have little confidence in any teachers who operate at such a 'professional' distance.

ATTITUDES NEEDED TO WORK EFFECTIVELY WITH PARENTS

In contrast to the negative views of parents which are described above, the attitudes which teachers need in order to work effectively with parents are ones which will help them develop productive partnerships. To bring this about teachers need to communicate to parents the attitudes of *genuineness*, *respect* and *empathy* suggested by Carl Rogers (1980). They must be *genuine* in their relationships with parents; that is, they should come across as real people with their own strengths and weaknesses. For example, they should always be prepared to say that they 'don't know' when this is the case. Hiding behind a professional facade of competence is not in anyone's interest. Teachers also need to show *respect* for parents: parents' opinions and requests should always be given serious consideration. In the final analysis parents' wishes should be respected even if they run counter to the views of teachers, since it is parents who have the long-term responsibility for their children. Most importantly, teachers need to develop *empathy* with parents: they should try to see the child's situation from the point of view of the parents. If teachers can develop an empathic understanding of the parents' position then it is much more likely that a productive parent–professional partnership will evolve.

Another important attitude which teachers need to have is hopeful but realistic views about the likely progress and eventual prognosis of the children with whom they work. Parents need teachers to be optimistic but objective about their children's development. They need teachers to be people of integrity who will not shy away from being open and honest with them, but will do this with sensitivity. In addition, teachers need to communicate the attitude that nothing is hopeless and that every situation can be improved, even if perhaps not all of the problems experienced by children or parents can be completely solved.

KNOWLEDGE NEEDED TO WORK EFFECTIVELY WITH PARENTS

If teachers do exhibit some negative attitudes towards parents instead of the positive attitudes discussed above, then it is hardly surprising since the majority of them would have received little or no input on working with parents on their initial training courses or as a part of any subsequent in-service training. Their attitudes towards parents would therefore have been influenced by those of senior colleagues and the community in which they live.

Fortunately, in the past twenty years there has been a substantial growth in the number of publications on parental involvement, and there is now a large number of books and articles on the topic which provide information for teachers. One aim of this book is to highlight the knowledge required by teachers to work effectively with parents which is over and above that which they require for effectively teaching children. There are several aspects of this additional knowledge.

First and foremost, teachers must have a good knowledge of strategies and techniques for working effectively with parents. Teachers need to have a good understanding of parents' perspectives; that is, they must be able to see and appreciate parents' points of view. Teachers must also be aware of family dynamics and be able to view all pupils within the context of their families. In addition, teachers need to know specifically what they can do to help parents of children with various types of difficulties, such as those with disabilities and illnesses as well as children affected by bereavement and family breakdown (see Chapters 7 and 8). Teachers also need to have adequate knowledge of how to work effectively with parents who present particular difficulties (see Chapter 9). Teachers need to be knowledgeable about the range of services and other resources which are available to parents. They need to be sufficiently aware of the beliefs and customs of the ethnic groups with which they work to be able to adapt their interventions so that they are culturally appropriate (Collins *et al.*, 1993).

SKILLS NEEDED TO WORK EFFECTIVELY WITH PARENTS

In addition to communicating appropriate attitudes and possessing relevant knowledge, in order to work effectively with parents, teachers need to have good interpersonal skills. An essential part of this is the possession of basic listening and counselling skills (Turnbull and Turnbull, 1986). Other interpersonal skills required by teachers include the assertion skills needed for working with parents and for collaborating with colleagues. Listening, counselling and assertion skills are discussed in Chapter 5.

Teachers also need the organizational and communication skills necessary for maintaining contact with parents through meetings, home visits, letters and telephone calls. These forms of contact are discussed in Chapter 3. In addition, teachers need the skills required for involving parents in their children's educational programmes such as in home–school reading schemes or home–school behaviour programmes. These programmes are discussed in Chapter 4. Finally, teachers need group leadership skills so that they can organize various group experiences for parents, such as parent education programmes. These are discussed in Chapter 6.

PARENTAL RIGHTS IN EDUCATION

The benefits of involving parents in their children's education first gained widespread acknowledgement from teachers in the UK in the 1960s following publication of the Plowden Report (DES, 1967) and reports on the projects conducted in educational priority areas, most of which involved working closely with parents. Legislation enacted in the UK in the last twenty years has had the effect of increasing the importance of parental involvement in education since parents' rights have been substantially extended (Statham *et al.*, 1989; Wolfendale, 1992). The additional rights given to parents in the UK during this period are summarized below.

1980 Education Act

In this legislation parents were granted the right to choose the school they want to send their children to. Parents were also given the right to be represented on the governing bodies of schools. In addition, school governors and local education authorities (LEAs) were required to provide written information to parents on such things as admission criteria, the curriculum, examination results, discipline, and school organization.

1981 Education Act

This Act gave parents the right to request the LEA to conduct a formal assessment of their children if they are suspected of having special educational needs. It requires parent involvement in the assessment process and in annual reviews of their children's progress. It also gives parents the right to appeal against LEA decisions about their children. Further, it made it clear that parents' wishes should be taken into account when deciding whether or not to integrate children with special needs into ordinary schools.

1986 Education Act

The first of two Acts passed in 1986 required increased parental representation on the governing bodies of schools. Governors were required to present an annual report to parents and to have a meeting with parents at the school in order to discuss the report.

1988 Education Act

This Act granted parents the right to send their children to any school of their choice so long as it has room for them. It also required that parents are sent an annual report on their children's progress. In addition it gave schools the opportunity of opting out of LEA control if a majority of parents voted in favour of this.

1992 Education Act

This Act set out new procedures for the inspection of schools, in which parents have an increased role. Parents have the right to meet with inspectors before the inspection to discuss any issues they wish. School staff and governors are not allowed to be present unless their children attend the school. Also, all parents are sent a questionnaire by the inspectors asking for their comments on the school. In addition, inspectors meet with parents to discuss a wide range of issues concerning schools, including the way schools involve parents in the identification and asssessment of special educational needs and annual reviews of Statements (Stone, 1993). Finally, parents have the right to receive a summary report on the results of the school inspection.

1993 Education Act

The code of practice on special educational needs, which provides guidance on the implementation of the 1993 Act, emphasizes the importance for schools of establishing partnerships with parents. It requires that schools should have written *policy and procedures* for:

- acting on parental concerns;
- involving parents when teachers express concerns about their child;
- incorporating parents' views in assessment and reviews of progress.

In addition, it requires that schools ensure that parents have *access* to this information by providing:

- information in the community languages spoken by parents for whom English is not their first language;
- information on tape for parents who have literacy difficulties;
- a parents' room or other arrangements to help parents feel comfortable about coming to the school.

The effect of the 1993 Education Act was therefore to further strengthen parental influence over the education of their children.

The increasing emphasis on parents' rights which has evolved through the above Education Acts means that schools can no longer afford *not* to work closely with parents. Of course, most schools already involve parents to some extent, in a variety of ways. Typical roles which parents fulfil in schools are discussed below.

PARENTAL ROLES IN EDUCATION

Eight ways which schools typically involve parents have been described by Morgan (1993) as:

1. recipients of information;
2. governors;
3. helpers;
4. fundraisers;
5. experts;
6. co-educators;
7. clients;
8. consultants.

These parental roles are discussed below.

Recipients of information

Parents have traditionally been on the receiving end of a variety of information from schools. There has been information about the school, such as what it offers to pupils and what it requires from pupils and their parents. There has also been information about the progress and behaviour of the pupils which has been conveyed to parents by means of annual reports and parent–teacher meetings. Following the 1992 and 1993 Education Acts there has been a marked increase in the amount of information conveyed to parents. For example, at the completion of school inspections parents are sent a report summarizing the findings of the inspection team. Therefore, an important role of parents is to be able to deal appropriately with the increasing amount of information they receive from schools.

Governors

As noted above, the role of parents as school governors has increased substantially in the UK in recent years. The 1980 Education Act required that the governing bodies of schools must include two parents. The 1986 Act extended this by prescribing that the number of parent governors should vary according to the size of the school, such that small schools would have two parents and large schools would have five parents. The 1988, 1992 and 1993 Acts have increased the duties of school governors. Therefore, recent years have seen a significant increase in the number of parents acting as school governors and a parallel increase in their influence on what goes on in schools. Unfortunately, these changes have generally not been accompanied by opportunities for parent governors to receive the training necessary for them to fulfil their roles competently (Scott, 1993).

Helpers

Many parents are involved in schools as voluntary helpers. Parents fulfil a wide range of helping roles including such activities as preparing classroom materials, listening to children read, and accompanying classes on a school visit. Parents also help by sharing particular skills which they have developed such as craft activities or specialist knowledge of a particular subject.

The use of parent helpers varies widely from school to school. I have visited some schools in which highly effective volunteer programmes have been running. However, in many schools parent helpers remain a largely untapped resource. This is probably because some teachers are put off such schemes by the fact that a small minority of parents who offer to help will create difficulties, perhaps by overstepping their role or by upsetting pupils or other parents. However, this is a reason for being careful in setting up and monitoring parent helper schemes, not for avoiding this aspect of parent involvement altogether. This potential difficulty perhaps explains why the best programmes I have seen have been tightly organized, with the helping tasks carefully specified and the programmes closely monitored by teachers.

Fundraisers

Raising money for the school by such means as cake stalls and fun runs has long been an important role which parents have played in the schools which their children have attended. It is probably of even greater importance in these times when less money is forthcoming from governments, and schools are expected to raise funds for items such as computers which many people regard as essential equipment in today's world.

In the past, fundraising was viewed by some teachers as the most important or perhaps even the only role which parents should play in schools. The main aim of parent–teacher associations was often considered to be fundraising. This is now not so much the case in most countries in which parents are being expected to fulfil other roles in schools.

Experts

A key contribution which most parents make to the functioning of schools is by providing teachers with valuable information about their children. This is particularly important for parents who have children with special needs. Parents need to pass on to teachers information about their children's difficulties, about any medication which they take and about family circumstances. Parents also need to inform teachers about such things as the likely effects of a family bereavement or a medical condition on the child's behaviour.

It is only recently that parents are beginning to be considered to be the experts on their children. In the past, professionals have tended to undervalue the knowledge which parents have of their children. This has resulted in many parents feeling frustrated that teachers have tended to talk *at* them rather than listen to what they have to say. This situation is changing and it is now realized by many teachers that, while they are the experts on education, parents are the experts on their children.

Co-educators

Many parents are now involved in projects which cast them in the role of co-educators of their children along with teachers. The involvement of parents ranges from such activities as checking homework diaries, through listening to children read, to highly structured parental involvement schemes (Topping, 1995). Home–school programmes have been reported in a wide range of curriculum areas such as reading, maths, science and European awareness, in addition to programmes which focus on children's behaviour. Acting as a co-educator is a key role for parents and is one which more and more of them are wanting to play. The involvement of parents as co-educators is discussed in Chapter 4.

Clients

Since the advent of open enrolment and Local Management of Schools parents' roles as clients or consumers have come to the fore. Parents now have a much bigger say in deciding which school their children will attend. These changes have meant that schools now view parents as potential customers whom they must attract to the school and for whom they may need to compete with other schools. Now that schools have a vested interest in attracting parents and keeping them satisfied, greater importance is attached to the need for all teachers to develop effective working relationships with parents.

Consultants

One consequence of the 1992 Education Act is that parents are being cast in the role of consultants to schools. As stated earlier, this Act requires that, as a part of the school inspection process, parents are to be consulted about how well the school functions, both by a questionnaire sent to their homes and by the opportunity to attend a meeting with the inspectors. Areas of concern can then be investigated by the inspection team. This represents a major change from the past when parents tended to be consulted about peripheral issues such as school uniforms but not about central aspects of the school such as the curriculum and the maintenance of discipline. Schools therefore need to be much more aware of how they are viewed by parents and of what parents see as strengths and weaknesses in the school's organization so that they can respond to these.

SUMMARY AND CONCLUSIONS

This book is aimed at helping teachers improve parental involvement in schools. This first chapter has provided a rationale for this enterprise and outlined the major attitudes, skills and knowledge which teachers need to develop. It is considered that, because of the widely varying roles which parents can play in schools and the increases in parental rights, both of which have been discussed in this chapter, it has become essential for each school to develop an appropriate philosophy and policy on working with parents (Wolfendale, 1992). Such a policy needs to be clear about parents' rights to participate in various aspects of school life. It needs to embody the idea of a working relationship based on the equality of value of contributions from parents and teachers. This involves acknowledging the different responsibilities but shared accountability of both teachers and parents within a working alliance formed on behalf of children. It also needs to embody the concept of equal opportunities for involvement of parents from a wide range of cultural backgrounds. This involves ensuring that all necessary means are used to overcome language barriers and that teachers avoid being judgemental when they encounter parents with different values and attitudes to child rearing.

In the following chapter, various approaches to working with parents are discussed and a model is presented which can be used to facilitate the design and implementation of school policy on parental involvement in order to provide a guide to professional practice with parents.

Chapter 2

Model for Parental Involvement

There is an exercise I like to begin with when leading workshops on parental involvement with teachers or with mixed groups of parents and teachers. I divide participants into groups, with about ten members in each. Each group takes the perspective of either parents or teachers. I then announce the task, which for the groups taking the perspective of parents is to discuss and report back on *'What we want from teachers'* and for the groups taking the perspective of teachers is to discuss and report back on *'What we want from parents'*.

I have used this exercise in various parts of the world including England, New Zealand, Barbados and India. No matter where I have done it, the responses have been remarkably similar from both teacher and parent perspectives. The usual result is a lively and vociferous discussion which highlights the difference in views and needs between teachers and parents. I have summarized the typical responses below.

The main things that parents want from teachers are as follows. They want:

- teachers to consult them more and listen to their points of view;
- a more open/approachable attitude from teachers;
- teachers to be willing to admit it if they don't know something;
- teachers to contact them if they suspect their child has a problem of any kind;
- teachers to treat all children with respect;
- teachers to make allowances for individual differences between children;
- teachers to identify and attempt to remediate learning difficulties;
- to discuss their children's progress at effective parent–teacher conferences;
- teachers to correct classwork and homework regularly;
- regular detailed reports on their children's progress;
- more teachers to be involved with parent–teacher associations (PTAs);
- teachers to use them more as a resource in the school.

The main things teachers want from parents are as follows. They want parents to:

- be open with them about children's special needs or health problems;
- tell them about any home circumstances which could affect pupils;
- co-operate in reinforcing school discipline at home;
- help reinforce the school programme at home through such things as supervising homework or listening to children read;
- teach children what is expected of them at school;
- have realistic expectations of what their children are capable of doing;
- attend PTA meetings;
- attend meetings with teachers to discuss children's progress;
- read and acknowledge reports and letters sent home;
- make sure the school has up-to-date address and phone details in case they need to be contacted during the day;
- keep children home if they are not well;
- volunteer to help out in various ways in school.

It is clear from this list that there are some differences in the expectations of parents and teachers, but there are also many similarities and complementary expectations. For example, teachers would like parents to be more open with them and parents want teachers to listen to them and consult them more. Also, teachers want parents to do more voluntary work in schools and parents say they are willing to do this. In addition, parents and teachers both reinforce the importance of parent–teacher conferences and PTA meetings.

The key value of this exercise to the participants is that it clarifies expectations on both sides. In most workshops there is genuine surprise on the part of many teachers and parents regarding some of the expectations placed on them. This highlights the necessity for more consideration to be given to the relationship between teachers and parents since it seems that assumptions are made on both sides without these being made explicit. This raises the issue of how parents and teachers should relate to each other. In order to illuminate this, various approaches to parent–teacher relationships will be discussed next.

APPROACHES TO PARENT–TEACHER RELATIONSHIPS

There are various approaches to parent–teacher relationships, each defined by a different set of assumptions, goals and strategies. These approaches range from those which attempt to minimize parental involvement to others which actively promote it. The approaches can be conceptualized in the form of models for the practice of parental involvement. The six most common models are the protective, expert, transmission, curriculum-enrichment, consumer, and partnership models.

Protective model

In the protective model (Swap, 1993) the main aim is to avoid conflict between teachers and parents by separating teaching and parenting functions. The education of children is carried out at school by teachers. The parents' role is to make sure children get to school on time with the correct equipment. Parental involvement in schools is seen as an unnecessary and potentially damaging interference in the efficient education of children. Swap considers that this approach is the most common model of parent–teacher relationships.

Expert model

In the expert model (Cunnningham and Davis, 1985) teachers regard themselves as the experts on all aspects of the development and education of children, whereas parents' views are accorded little credence. Teachers maintain control over decisions, while the parents' role is to receive information and instructions about their children. A major problem with this approach is that it encourages parents to be submissive and dependent on teachers. Parents are reluctant to question teachers' decisions and tend to lose faith in their own competence. Another problem is that, because teachers do not make use of the rich source of knowledge parents have about their children, they tend to overlook important problems or abilities which the children have. In addition, teachers working within the expert model will not be aware of any difficulties which parents themselves might experience. All these factors increase the possibility that parents will be dissatisfied with the service they get from teachers who adopt this approach.

Transmission model

In the transmission model (Swap, 1993) parents' help is enlisted in order to support the goals of the school. The model is employed by teachers who regard themselves as the main sources of expertise on children but who recognize the benefits of using parents as a resource. They consider that some of their expertise can be transmitted from them to parents so that parents can carry out some form of intervention with their children. A well-known example of this approach in the field of education is a paired reading programme in which parents are trained to help their children with reading at home (Topping, 1995).

In this model the teacher remains in control and decides on the interventions to be used but does accept that parents can play an important part in facilitating their children's progress. Therefore, there is more likelihood that parents' views will be considered and their concerns addressed. However, in order to use this approach teachers do need additional skills such as techniques for effectively guiding parents and the interpersonal skills required for establishing productive working relationships with them. These factors will increase the likelihood of parents being satisfied with the service they receive and reduce the tendency for them to become dependent on teachers.

The danger of this approach is the assumption that all parents can and should take on the role of acting as a resource. This risks overburdening some parents by placing excessive demands on them to carry out intervention programmes with their children. The chances of this happening are increased for children with special needs since several different professionals, such as speech therapists, psychologists and teachers may all be expecting parents to carry out intervention programmes in the home.

Curriculum-enrichment model

The goal of the curriculum-enrichment model (Swap, 1993) is to extend the school curriculum by incorporating parents' contributions. It is based on the assumption that parents have important expertise to contribute and that the interaction between parents and teachers around the implementation of the curriculum material will enhance the educational objectives of the school. The focus of parental involvement in this model is mainly on curriculum and instruction within schools. An example of an area of the curriculum for which this approach has been widely used is multicultural education. Parents from various ethnic, religious and cultural groups have been able to collaborate with teachers in order to develop and implement curricula which accurately reflect the history, values and views of the groups which they represent. But parents' input need not be restricted to multicultural education. For example, Swap reports a project in which two parents with science degrees became involved in designing and teaching curriculum material in the area of science.

This model suggests a novel way of involving parents in children's learning which increases the resources available to the school and provides opportunities for parents and teachers to learn from each other. Its major drawback is that in order to implement this model it requires that teachers allow parents to have a major input in what is taught and how it is taught, which can be threatening to many teachers.

Consumer model

In the consumer model (Cunnningham and Davis, 1985) parents are regarded as being consumers of educational services. The teacher acts as a consultant while the parent decides what action is to be taken. The parent has control over the decision-making process while the teacher's role is to provide them with relevant information and a range of options from which to choose. Thus, in this approach, the teacher defers to parents, who are effectively placed in the expert role. The teacher's role is to listen to parents' views and help them choose from the alternatives available. Because parents are in control of the decision-making process in this approach they are likely to be much more satisfied with the service they receive, to feel more competent about their parenting and are also less likely to become dependent on professionals.

The danger of this approach is that, taken to its extreme, it can lead to an abdication of professional responsibility. I have seen this occur while working as an educational psychologist when a colleague adopted an extreme form of the consumer model. This psychologist would handle the selection of an appropriate educational placement for a child with special needs by simply showing parents around a variety of schools and classes and getting them to choose one. Without the benefit of relevant information and guidance about the likely advantages and disadvantages of each potential placement for the child in question, from the professional knowledgeable about how special needs can be most effectively met, parents were encouraged to make uninformed decisions which may not have been in their children's best interests. In this way parents were placed in the role of experts on how their children's special needs could be met. This seems to me to be just as inappropriate as professionals regarding themselves as experts on all aspects of children's functioning, and therefore adopting the expert model in their relationships with parents.

Partnership model

The most appropriate model for relationships between teachers and parents is considered to be one in which teachers are viewed as experts on education and parents are viewed as experts on their children. The relationship between teachers and parents can then be a partnership which involves the sharing of expertise and control in order to provide the optimum education for all children. Parents and teachers contribute different strengths to their relationship, thereby increasing the potency of the partnership. For example, most parents have strong emotional attachments to their children and therefore make excellent advocates for them. However, the emotional attachment also tends to make them somewhat subjective when considering their children's abilities and needs, which is why the objectivity that teachers bring to the partnership is so important.

An essential aspect of the partnership envisaged is that it must be based on mutual respect. For example, it requires parents and teachers to listen to each other and give due consideration to each other's views. This partnership also requires a long-term commitment to a wide range of activities involving both teachers and parents. It also must encompass a sharing of planning and decision-making responsibilities (Swap, 1993). In this way effective collaborative working relationships between teachers and parents can be established. The four key elements of such a partnership are: two-way communication; mutual support; joint decision-making; and enhancement of learning at school and at home.

Two-way communication

There must be open, two-way communication between parents and teachers with both partners listening to each other so that, for example, parents can share information on their children's needs and teachers can provide information about children's progress at school.

Mutual support
Teachers and parents must support one another's efforts; for example, teachers can provide guidance on how parents can help children at home and parents can act as voluntary helpers at school.

Joint decision-making
Teachers and parents need to be involved in joint problem-solving and decision-making at the levels of: individual children; the classroom; and the school.

Enhancement of learning
Parents and teachers need to develop a range of opportunities for parents to be involved in promoting their children's learning both at school and at home.

However, having the partnership model as an overall guide does not preclude the use of interventions based on the other approaches when they would be more appropriate. For example, the transmission model correctly provides the underlying rationale for many of the parent involvement projects, such as home–school reading schemes, which are described in Chapter 4. Also, the adoption of the expert model is justified in prescribing treatment, such as personal therapy or parenting skills programmes, for parents who have subjected their children to physical, emotional or sexual abuse (Morgan, 1985; Walker *et al.*, 1988).

In fact, some interventions, such as the parent education programmes described in Chapter 6, can be organized from different perspectives depending on the group of parents to be involved. That is, they can be organized from the perspective of the consumer model with parents stipulating what guidance or input they would like. Alternatively, they can be organized from the perspective of the expert model with teachers specifying what parents need to learn. For example, parents of children with special needs may be able and willing to select suitable input (consumer model), whereas parents who have subjected their children to some form of abuse are likely to need professionals to decide what input would be most beneficial (expert).

Therefore, although there must be enough flexibility to enable other models to be used when necessary, it is considered that the partnership model is generally the most appropriate perspective from which to develop constructive parental involvement. In this model, teachers are aware of addressing parents' needs and of acknowledging the various ways parents can contribute to the development and education of their children. This will facilitate the development of effective partnerships between parents and teachers. In order for such partnerships to become more than just lofty ideals, the concept needs to be developed into a model for parent involvement which is designed to guide practice. This is considered in the next section.

THE NEED FOR A MODEL OF PARENT INVOLVEMENT

The evolution of parent involvement worldwide has tended to be practice-led rather than being guided by theory or policy (Atkin *et al.*, 1988). Many examples of interesting parent involvement projects are in existence around the world and useful models are available for various types of parent involvement. Also, numerous books have been written with the intention of providing teachers with the knowledge necessary to build effective relationships with parents (e.g. Bastiani, 1987, 1988, 1989; Berger, 1991; Blamires *et al.*, 1997; Cyster *et al.*, 1979; Gargiulo, 1985; Griffiths and Hamilton, 1984; Harding and Pike, 1988; Hornby, 1995a; Jowett *et al.*, 1991; Kroth, 1985; Lombana, 1983; McConkey, 1985; Pugh and De'Ath, 1984; Seligman, 1979; Simpson, 1996; Stewart, 1986; Sullivan, 1988; Tizard *et al.*, 1981; Topping, 1986; Wolfendale, 1983, 1992).

However, none of these books has focused specifically on what teachers can do to improve parental involvement in their schools, which is the central theme of this book. As a first step towards this goal it is necessary to develop a vision of what effective parental involvement would look like. The best way to do this is to produce a comprehensive theoretical model for parental involvement. Such a model can then be used to provide teachers with a framework with which to formulate overall policy and plans for working with parents. The model will also enable each school to conduct an audit of its current practice of parental involvement in order to ensure that, as far as possible, parents' needs are being met and their potential contributions are being utilized.

MODEL FOR PARENT INVOLVEMENT

The theoretical model for parental involvement described below was developed by combining and adapting existing models (e.g. Bastiani, 1989; Kroth, 1985; Lombana, 1983; Wolfendale, 1992) and by gaining feedback from numerous groups of parents and teachers. The model was originally devised with teachers of children with special needs in mind (Hornby, 1989) but it was subsequently realized that, with slight adaptations, it was equally applicable to all teachers (Hornby, 1990). The model for parent involvement is presented in Figure 2.1.

The model consists of two pyramids, one representing a hierarchy of parents' needs, the other a hierarchy of parents' strengths or possible contributions. Both pyramids demonstrate visually the different levels of needs and contributions of parents. Thus, while all parents have some needs and some potential contributions which can be utilized, a smaller number have an intense need for guidance, or the capability of making an extensive contribution. The model also shows that, for parents' needs at a higher level, more time and expertise are required by teachers in order to meet these needs. Similarly, the parents who make a greater contribution require a higher level of expertise and time available.

Each of the components of the model will now be outlined, and the

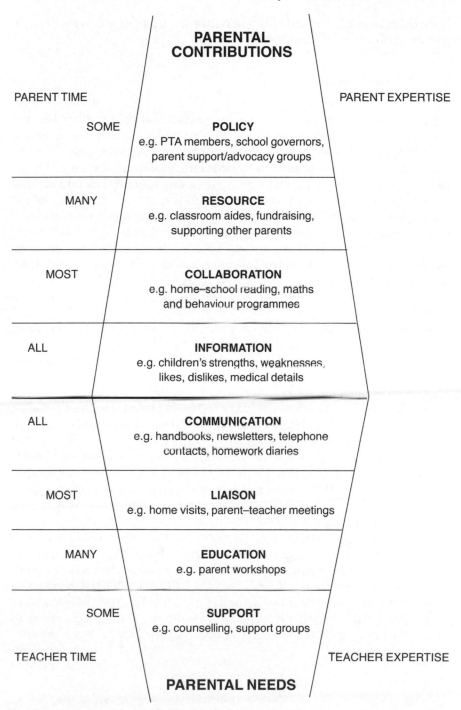

Figure 2.1: Model for parent involvement

knowledge and skills needed by teachers in order to participate in each type of parent involvement will be identified.

Contributions by parents

Information

All parents can contribute valuable information about their children because they have known them throughout their lives and have been the ones who have participated in all previous contacts with professionals in order to assess and plan for meeting their children's needs. Information concerning children's likes and dislikes, strengths and weaknesses, along with any relevant medical details can be gathered by teachers at parent–teacher meetings. Making full use of parents' knowledge of their children not only leads to more effective professional practice, it also makes parents feel that they have been listened to and that an active interest has been taken in their children. Therefore, teachers need to develop good listening and interviewing skills (Atkin *et al.*, 1988; Seligman, 1979).

Collaboration

Most parents are willing and able to contribute more than just information. They are able to collaborate with teachers by reinforcing classroom programmes at home, such as in home–school reading programmes (Topping, 1995). However, some parents, at some times, are not able to carry out work at home with their children. This can be very frustrating for teachers since they realize that collaboration between home and school results in children making greater progress, so that children whose parents do not work closely with them are likely to develop more slowly. However, I have come to believe that teachers have to accept that some parents at some points in time are simply not able to collaborate in this way. It is probably because their resources are already fully committed in coping with their children at home, so they are not able to do anything extra. At a later time family circumstances may change and parents may then want to become more involved in their children's education. Teachers must respect parents' rights to make this decision in consideration of the wider needs of their families. So, while involvement in home–school programmes, or other requests for parents to carry out work with their children at home, should always be offered to all parents, including those who have not collaborated in the past, it should be expected that a small proportion of parents will not participate. Therefore, teachers need the skills of collaborating with parents in a flexible partnership in which parents' choices are respected.

Resource

Many parents have the time and ability to act as voluntary teacher aides, either assisting in the classroom, or in the preparation of materials, or in fundraising. Others may have special skills which they can contribute, such as helping prepare newsletters, in craft activities, or in curriculum areas in which they have a special talent. Some parents may have the time, skills and knowledge to provide support to other parents either informally or perhaps through participation in self-help or support groups.

In these times of contracting professional resources teachers should make sure that they make optimum use of this valuable voluntary resource. It is often the case that parents also benefit from acting as a resource. They may acquire knowledge which is helpful to their understanding of their own children. In addition, they are often observed to gain in confidence through helping at school and go on to further their own education. In order to enable as many parents as possible to act as a resource to the school, teachers need practical management and communication skills (Kroth, 1985).

Policy

Some parents are able to contribute their expertise through membership of parent or professional organizations. This includes being a school governor, a lay inspector, a member of the PTA, or being involved in a parent support or advocacy group. Others have the time and ability to provide in-service training by speaking at conferences or workshops, or by writing about their experiences (e.g. Featherstone, 1981). Teachers should continually be on the look-out for parents who can contribute in this way so that their abilities can be used to the full.

Needs of parents

Communication

All parents need to have effective channels of communication with their children's teachers. They need information about the organization and requirements of the school as it affects their child. They need to know when their children are having difficulties and what the school is going to do to address these. That is, parents need to know about their rights and responsibilities. This can be provided through handbooks or regular newsletters written especially for parents.

Parents need to feel that they can contact the school at any time when they have a concern about their child. Some parents prefer to communicate by telephone, others would rather call in to see the teacher face to face, while still others find that contact through written notes or home–school diaries suits them best. Therefore, educators need to develop effective written and oral communication skills and to ensure that a wide range of communication options are open to parents. However, the most important factor in maintaining good communication is the openness to parents which schools demonstrate through their contacts with parents. The attitude of choice has often been referred to as an 'open door policy' in which parents feel comfortable about contacting or going into the school when they have a concern (Bastiani, 1987).

Liaison

Most parents want to know how their children are getting on at school. They want to find out what their children have achieved and whether they are having any difficulties. They regard teachers as the main source of information on their children's performance at school and therefore need to have a working partnership with them. Teachers can facilitate this by keeping in regular contact with parents through such means as telephone calls, home visits, home–school notebooks, weekly report cards and by meeting with parents at school. These strategies are discussed in detail in Chapter 3.

Teachers are often disappointed that some parents do not come to parent–teacher meetings at school, thereby giving the impression that they are not interested in how their children are getting on. In my experience, there are usually other reasons for them not turning up, such as the difficulties involved in getting a baby-sitter, the overwhelming demands of looking after their family, or anxieties about coming to school related to the negative experiences they themselves may have had at school. It is important, then, for teachers to find other ways of liaising with these parents, perhaps by regular telephone contacts or home visits.

Therefore, teachers need to develop the skills of conducting formal and informal meetings with parents. In addition, they need to offer a range of options for liaison with parents so that those who do not feel comfortable coming to formal meetings with teachers have other forms of regular contact made available to them (Simpson, 1996).

Education

Many parents are interested in participating in parent education (or parent training) programmes aimed at promoting their children's progress or managing their behaviour. Parent education can be conducted individually (White and Cameron, 1988) or in parent groups or workshops (Topping, 1986). Some parents will not want to take part in such programmes, for a variety of reasons. There will be those who, at a certain point in time, feel confident about the way they are parenting their children and don't see the need for parent education. Later, when their children reach a different developmental stage they may think differently. For other parents, there will be practical difficulties such as arranging baby-sitters or transport. However, in my experience, a substantial number of parents are interested in being involved in parent education workshops and most of those who do participate get a tremendous amount out of it. Ideally then, opportunities for taking part in either individual or group parent education should be made available to all parents.

It seems that the most effective format for parent education is one which combines guidance about promoting children's development with opportunities for parents to discuss their concerns (Pugh and De'Ath, 1984). Parent education programmes which involve a group of parents, and employ a workshop format, easily lend themselves to providing a combination of educational input and sharing of concerns. This type of format enables parents to learn new skills and gain confidence through talking to other parents and teachers (Hornby and Murray, 1983). To be involved in parent education, therefore, teachers need to have the listening and counselling skills discussed in Chapter 5 and the skills of group facilitation discussed in Chapter 6.

Support

Some parents, at some times, are in need of supportive counselling, even though they may not actually request it. This support can be provided either individually or in group counselling sessions. Although such support should be available to all parents, the majority of parents seldom need extensive counselling. The fact is, that if parents have good channels of communication and regular liaison with teachers, coupled with the opportunity to receive guidance about their children whenever they need it, then only a few of them will need counselling at any particular time.

   Whereas most parents are reluctant to seek the help of professional counsellors, they will approach their children's teachers in search of guidance or counselling for the problems which concern them. Teachers should therefore have a level of basic counselling skills sufficient to be good listeners and to help parents solve everyday problems. They should also have the knowledge necessary to be able to refer parents on to professional counsellors when problems raised are beyond their level of competence.

USING THE MODEL TO GUIDE PARENT INVOLVEMENT PRACTICE

Using the model described above a comprehensive scheme of parental involvement can be designed to suit each school. The model can be used to generate a checklist designed to ensure that procedures are in place to meet parents' needs and to make sure that parents' potential contributions are being fully utilized. The checklist which follows has been adapted from a previous checklist on parent–professional relationships (Mittler, undated). It provides an example of the kinds of questions which teachers need to ask themselves when reviewing their school's policy and practice regarding parent involvement. Each level of the model for parent involvement will now be considered in turn and questions posed for teachers to consider.

Policy

* *Does the school have a separate written policy on parent involvement?* Does the policy clearly specify parents' rights and responsibilities and is it included in material distributed to all parents and teachers?
* *Have parents been involved in the formulation of this policy?* For example, have the PTA or parent governors had input into the policy design process?
* *What monitoring procedures are in place to ensure that the policy is implemented?* For example, how is feedback obtained from parents?

- *Is there an active parent–teacher association (PTA) at the school?* What can be done to encourage more parents to participate in PTA activities?
- *What involvement do parents have in discussions about the aims of the school, the curriculum and other issues such as parent–teacher relationships?* For example, are parents' views sought about the school's policy for meeting special educational needs?
- *Is there a room set aside for parents' use?* Do parents use a spare classroom, or can the staffroom be used by parents during lesson times?
- *What means are there for encouraging parents to become school governors?* Are all teachers on the look-out for parents who would be effective in this role?
- *Are parents involved in in-service training?* For example, have parents of children with special educational needs been invited to talk about their experiences, expectations, needs and possible contributions?
- *Who is responsible for ensuring that parents with a particular talent for leadership are identified and encouraged to put their abilities to use?* Who identifies parents who could contribute to the school in capacities such as on the PTA or governing body?

Resource

- *In what kinds of activities does the school welcome help from parents?* Are parents used to listen to children read or to assist in teaching or in preparing classroom materials?
- *How are parents informed about the ways in which they can help at the school?* Is there a parents' handbook or a regular newsletter?
- *How is voluntary help from parents organized within the school?* For example, is a particular member of staff assigned to co-ordinate the help or is it seen as the responsibility of each teacher?

Collaboration

- *How do parents contribute to the assessment of their child's needs?* For example, by being asked for their observations or by completing developmental checklists.
- *How are the results of school assessments communicated to parents?* Are individual parent–teacher meetings scheduled?
- *What input do parents have in deciding the goals and teaching priorities for their children?* For example, do parents discuss with teachers the emphasis which should be placed on developing basic academic skills or social skills, as part of the personal and social education curriculum?
- *How are parents encouraged to reinforce school programmes at home?* For example, are they expected to participate in a paired reading scheme?
- *Are parents given a choice about the level of their involvement at home with their children?* Is there discussion with parents beforehand so that they are

not pressured into projects which they cannot afford the time or energy to carry out?.
- *How are parents of children with special needs involved in developing their child's Individual Educational Plan (IEP)?* For example, do they attend all the meetings and have a chance to discuss their child with any outside specialists involved, such as peripatetic teachers, educational psychologists or speech therapists?
- *How is parental involvement in reviews of their children's progress optimized?* For example, by obtaining their observations beforehand and being an active member of the review team.

Information

- *How is information on children's special needs, medical conditions and relevant family circumstances, gathered from parents?* Are home visits used in addition to parent–teacher meetings at school?
- *How is relevant information from parents disseminated to all members of staff who work with their children?* What systems are used to record, and communicate to teachers, information about such things as children's special needs and the medication they require?
- *What use is made of parents' insights on their children?* For example, parents' knowledge of their children's strengths and weaknesses, likes and dislikes, or how they respond to different approaches.

Communication

- *What activities are used to ensure that all parents establish contact with the school?* Are performances or exhibitions of work by the pupils, social occasions or talks by well-known invited speakers used to attract large numbers of parents into the school?
- *How does the school pass on information to parents about their rights and responsibilities and about school organization?* For example, is this information disseminated by means of newsletters and handbooks specifically aimed at parents or by holding meetings at which school policies are discussed?
- *Does the school have balanced procedures for contacting parents?* That is, are parents contacted to inform them of their children's achievements as well as their difficulties or are they only contacted when there is a problem?
- *Does a member of staff visit families before pupils start to attend the school?* Are home visits scheduled when children are changing schools, moving from primary to secondary school, or being re-integrated following a period in a special school?
- *What guidelines are available for parents on visiting the school to talk over a concern with their children's teachers?* For example, do they have to go through the headteacher, make an appointment directly with the teacher, or just come in whenever they can?

- *What channels of communication are there between parents and teachers?* That is, can parents choose to telephone, write notes or call in to the school as and when necessary?

Liaison

- *What are the frequency and purpose of parent–teacher meetings?* For example, are parents invited to attend termly or yearly meetings to review their children's progress?
- *Do parents regularly receive home visits?* Are home visits made at least once a year, or only when there is a problem? Are visits made by class teachers or senior members of staff? Is there flexibility in the time of day used so that both parents can be present?
- *How are home–school diaries used?* For example, are they used for all children or just for ones with special educational needs or for those with behavioural difficulties? Are diaries used daily or weekly?
- *What kinds of formal reports are sent home?* Are reports sent termly or yearly? Are progress reports sent separately to records of achievement?

Education

- *Are parents invited into the school to observe teaching in progress?* For example, are they invited to observe either their own child or other children in the school?
- *When are teachers available to provide guidance to parents?* Do teachers make home visits in order to provide guidance to parents or does this only occur in parent–teacher meetings at school?
- *Are parent workshops organized by the school?* For example, are there workshops for parents of children with reading difficulties or behaviour problems or for parents whose children are about to leave school?
- *Are parents informed about opportunities for parent education in the community?* Is information about parenting courses provided by adult education centres or universities made available to parents?

Support

- *How are parents given opportunities to discuss their concerns on a one-to-one basis?* For example, is this done on home visits or in specially scheduled parent–teacher meetings at school?
- *Are opportunities provided for parents to share their concerns with other parents?* For example, are parents introduced to other parents who have children with similar difficulties? Are they given the opportunity of attending group counselling programmes or parent workshops?
- *Do teachers know where to refer parents for supportive counselling?* Is there an awareness of services and groups within the local community

which can provide supportive counselling, such as social workers or self-help groups?
* *Are parents encouraged to participate in support groups and parent organizations outside the school?* For example, MENCAP or CRUSE.

SUMMARY AND CONCLUSIONS

The expectations of parents and teachers of each other which emerged from workshops in different parts of the world were presented in order to suggest that, in the past, insufficient attention has been paid to developing productive parent–teacher relationships. A review of professional approaches to working with parents based on various models was used to clarify the form of parent–teacher relationship which is considered to be the most productive. It was suggested that a theoretical model for parent involvement is needed in order to assist schools to design policies and procedures for involving parents. The model proposed addresses parents' needs and their potential contributions and suggests competences needed by teachers in order to ensure its successful implementation. The model is also used to generate a checklist of questions which schools can employ to evaluate their practice of parental involvement in order to identify strengths and areas which need further development.

Chapter 3

Improving Communication with Parents

When I am working with a group of teachers and they complain about the low levels of parental involvement in their schools, I like to get them to brainstorm ideas for improving this situation. I provide them with a concept map, either on paper or drawn on the blackboard or flip-chart, which is blank except for 'Strategies for involving parents' written in the circle in the middle. With a little prompting most groups come up with an excellent range of strategies to fill in the other circles on the map, as illustrated in Figure 3.1.

What this exercise suggests to me is that teachers often know what sort of activities will improve parental involvement in their schools but they lack the

Figure 3.1: Strategies for involving parents

knowledge of how to effectively put these into action. In order to provide the necessary information, this chapter reviews a variety of strategies available to teachers for communicating with parents and provides suggestions on how these can most effectively be used. Before beginning this task it is important to consider what preferences parents have for the various forms of involvement.

PARENT PREFERENCES

The limited amount of research which has focused on parental preferences for the various forms of involvement has generally found that most parents prefer communication with teachers to be *frequent* and *informal*. Turnbull and Turnbull (1986) reported the results of a survey conducted in the USA with 217 parents of children with a wide range of special needs. This found that 69 per cent of parents wanted to communicate with teachers by means of letters, 51 per cent by parent–teacher interviews, 45 per cent by telephone calls and only 19 per cent by home visits. When another group of parents in the USA were asked to rank twenty different common methods of home–school communication, the most popular methods were: directly approaching teachers by telephone or in person; and parent–teacher interviews (Cattermole and Robinson, 1985).

A similar survey of contact between home and school was conducted with 72 parents of children attending a special school for children with physical disabilities in the north of England (Young, 1991). This found that 46 per cent of parents had contact with the school at least weekly and 83 per cent had contact at least monthly. With regard to the preferred types of home–school communication, 69 per cent of parents wanted this to be by means of parent–teacher interviews, 67 per cent by telephone calls, 50 per cent by home visits, 47 per cent by home–school diaries and 40 per cent by means of letters. It was reassuring to note that when these parents were asked about the actual forms of contact which they had with staff at the school the percentages for the various types of contact were very similar to those above, except in the area of home visits. Surprisingly, only 15 per cent of parents had received home visits, whereas 50 per cent of parents indicated that they would have appreciated them.

It is clear from the findings of these surveys that there are a few common strategies but also differences among parents regarding their preferred methods of communicating with teachers. Therefore, it is important for schools to be able to offer parents a range of communication options. There are five main methods for developing and maintaining two-way communication between parents and teachers. These are:

1. informal contacts;
2. telephone contacts;
3. various forms of written communication;
4. parent–teacher meetings;
5. home visits.

These are now discussed in turn, starting with informal contacts.

INFORMAL CONTACTS

Informal contacts are a useful way of 'breaking the ice' in most forms of human relationships and this is also the case in relationships with parents. Such contacts provide a means whereby parents and teachers can meet each other as people with a mutual interest in building relationships on behalf of children, thereby helping to break down the barriers that often exist between school and home (Swap, 1993). Informal contacts are particularly important for parents of children newly enrolled at the school or when there has not been a high level of parent involvement at the school in the past. In the latter situation, teachers understandably become despondent when the attendance at more formal events, such as parents' evenings, is so poor. When this is the case it is often best to organize informal events in order to increase the numbers of parents having contact with the school and thereby establish the context necessary for the development of other forms of contact.

The organization of informal contacts is illustrated by the following descriptions of four different types of activities: school productions, open days, gala days, and outings into the local community.

School productions

The type of informal occasion guaranteed to achieve the maximum attendance of parents is one in which they see their children perform in some way or other. It is possible to organize activities so that all pupils are involved in such events as school concerts or Nativity plays and thereby ensure almost 100 per cent attendance of parents.

Open days

Another way to encourage a large proportion of parents to come into the school is to have an 'open day' or 'open evening' when parents can come along to see classes in progress and/or displays of their children's work.

Gala days

Events whose main aim is raising funds for the school, by having stalls which sell home-made food, and activities such as races for children and adults, also provide opportunities for teachers, parents and pupils to meet informally.

Outings

Class or year-group or even school outings to places such as local parks on weekends or at holiday times can attract large numbers of parents and other family members.

Ensuring success of informal events

Swap (1993) provides a list of suggestions for making informal occasions successful. These are outlined below.

Personal invitations
In addition to the event being advertised in the school newsletter, parents should receive individually addressed invitations, possibly produced and delivered by their children. Invitations should give at least two weeks' notice of the event so that parents can make the necessary arrangements. Then, two or three days before the event, reminder notes should be sent home with the children.

Facilitating attendance
The two major difficulties which parents experience in arranging to attend school events are with transportation and child care. Providing assistance in each of these areas will improve attendance rates. For example, organizing car pools or minibuses to pick up parents will enable some parents to come who otherwise wouldn't have been able to. Also, organizing child-care facilities or making the event suitable for the whole family to attend is likely to substantially increase attendance. Finally, it is worth bearing in mind that events planned for evenings and weekends are more likely to get fathers involved.

Welcoming atmosphere
The first step taken in any form of parental involvement should be to make parents feel welcome. For events held at the school it is important to make the school entrance and foyer as welcoming and comfortable as possible. Ideally, when parents first arrive they should be greeted and shown around by pupils or other parents. If this is not possible then directions to where the event is to be held should be clearly signposted.

Optimizing opportunities for informal communication
Careful planning is required to ensure that informal events do provide opportunities for parents and teachers to mix and talk with each other. Seating arrangements and planned activities should be organized to facilitate mixing rather than allowing people to sit with others they already know.

Providing food and drink
One of the best ways of promoting informal conversation is through arranging for food and drink at an event. There is something about eating and drinking with other people which helps to cement relationships and build rapport. Potluck meals when everyone brings a plate of home-cooked food are particularly good for this.

Evaluating activities
Inviting parents to formally and informally evaluate activities ensures that their feedback can be used to improve subsequent events.

TELEPHONE CONTACTS

Nowadays the vast majority of parents have a telephone: so most parents are quite comfortable about communicating with teachers by means of the telephone and many parents prefer to maintain contact with teachers in this way.

Parents phoning teachers

Many parents appreciate the opportunity of being able to phone teachers directly either at school or at home. However, there are difficulties associated with both of these options. The main problem with parents phoning teachers at school is that teachers should only have to leave their class to answer the telephone in absolute emergencies. So it is usually best to get the school secretary to take messages and tell parents that the teacher will phone back as soon as possible.

Some teachers may not be prepared to allow parents to phone them at home. This is perfectly understandable since they may feel the need to have some time to themselves, or with their own families, which work pressures do not impinge on. Other teachers may want to encourage parents to phone them at home in preference to being phoned at school. An alternative solution is to set a specified time of day or evening during the week when parents know the teacher will be at home and available to answer the phone.

Teachers phoning parents

Teachers should check whether some parents are at home during the day and others are happy to be phoned at work, in which case at least some of the calls could be made from school during the day. Otherwise, it means phoning parents in the evening in teachers' own time.

Whenever telephone calls are made to parents there are certain guidelines which it is wise to follow. The following guidelines were generated from reflecting on some of my successes and errors in phoning parents and from adapting the suggestions made by Turnbull and Turnbull (1986).

1. Identify yourself as their child's teacher when parents first answer.
2. Ask if it is a convenient time to talk or whether it would be better if you called back later.
3. Make a point of finding out the best time to call parents. Usually later in the evening, when children are in bed, is the most suitable time.
4. Use a written list of things you want to ask or tell parents which you have prepared beforehand.
5. Be concise and to the point. If an issue needs lengthy discussion it is better to do it face to face than on the phone.
6. Listen carefully to what the parent has to say, using the listening skills discussed in Chapter 5.
7. Give the parent time to ask you questions and to think about the things you have said.

8. If you don't have the information that parents want, suggest you will find out and get back to them as soon as possible.
9. Avoid relaying sensitive information by telephone. This is better done face to face so that parents' reactions can be gauged.
10. Always finish by thanking parents for their time and remind them that they can contact you any time they have a concern.

Other uses of the telephone

Two other uses of the telephone in working with parents are reported by Turnbull and Turnbull (1986). First, the *telephone tree* can be used as an efficient way to get information to parents. Once the list (or tree) of parents' names and phone numbers is circulated to all parents the teacher simply has to ring the first name on the list and parents then ring each other in turn to pass on the information. Variations on this system include the teacher phoning two parents who in turn phone another two parents. This continues until all parents have been contacted. An additional benefit of the telephone tree is that parents are encouraged to interact with one another, which may lead to supportive friendships being formed.

Second, an answerphone can be used to play *recorded daily messages* for parents who ring the school phone number in the evening or at the weekend. For example, messages can be recorded to tell parents about the activities the class have been involved in during the day, about the homework that has been set or to remind them about equipment needed for the following day. Turnbull and Turnbull report a study which found that children performed better on homework tasks using the system of recorded daily messages rather than the traditional homework diaries.

WRITTEN COMMUNICATION

Many parents prefer to communicate with teachers by means of letters. Other parents find that home–school diaries or notebooks are the best means of keeping them in contact with the school. In addition, newsletters and handbooks written especially for parents of children with special needs can keep parents in touch with what is happening at school. It is therefore clear that the written word provides an important means of communication between teachers and parents.

However, there are two major difficulties with this form of communication. First, if some of the pupils' parents do not have English as their first language then ideally every written communication to parents needs to be translated into their own languages. Second, it is important to remember that some parents have reading difficulties themselves. Therefore, written materials cannot be relied upon to communicate effectively with all parents. This also suggests that all written materials should use language which is simple and able to be understood by the majority of parents.

Handbooks

Most schools have prospectuses or brochures whose purpose is to inform new or prospective parents about the school's aims and organization. These tend to be general documents which focus on promoting positive features of the school and informing parents about the major school rules for pupils and policies for teaching (Bastiani, 1989). It has been suggested by Kroth (1985) that parents of children with special needs appreciate having a handbook written especially for them. The handbook should inform parents about their rights and responsibilities regarding their children, along with all the information they need in order to help them to be happy and successful at the school. For parents of children with special needs in ordinary schools, a handbook prepared for all parents who have children at the school may be able to meet their needs if it addresses the following aspects of school life.

Personnel
School staff, such as heads of year and the school's co-ordinator for special educational needs, should be listed along with their contact phone numbers, as well as those of outside specialists such as educational psychologists.

Policies
The school's policy for parental involvement and for meeting special needs should be clearly spelled out. This should include an explanation for parents of who to contact if they have a concern and of the best methods for making this contact.

School-wide procedures
School rules regarding dress and discipline should be briefly outlined and the specific procedures for rewarding effort and progress and for dealing with misbehaviour should be explained.

Classroom procedures
An indication of the materials and equipment pupils will need for various subjects should be included.

Transport
The arrangements for transporting pupils to and from school should be detailed.

Reports home
A description of the type and frequency of the progress reports parents will receive should be included.

Other information
Any other information which would be helpful to parents should be included, such as details of Adult Education classes relevant to parenting which are based at the school.

Newsletters

Newsletters regularly sent out to parents, typically once or twice a term, are a very good way of communicating with the majority of parents. Newsletters can be general ones which are addressed to all parents of children at the school, or more specific ones addressed to parents of children in a particular year, or just to the parents of children with special needs. Newsletters can include a variety of content including notices for forthcoming events, updates of ongoing school projects and invitations for parents to help at the school.

Letters and notes

Letters are a time-consuming means for communicating with parents. Therefore, it is generally better to use the other forms of communication described above for most purposes and only use letters for situations which require a more formal approach. For example, most schools will, as a last resort, use letters to express concern about a child's behaviour and invite parents to come to school to discuss the problem. However, this use of letters to deal with discipline problems should be balanced by a system of positive letters sent to parents to acknowledge a child's outstanding effort or progress.

In contrast to formal letters, teachers often find it useful to send brief handwritten notes home to parents via children's school bags. This can be a quick and effective way of getting a message to parents with whom teachers already have a good relationship, but it does have its drawbacks. Notes can sometimes become lost on the way home or can be overlooked when parents are emptying the school bag. Also, there is no record kept of what has been written.

Home–school diary

Many parents prefer to use a book for written communication between themselves and teachers. It is more difficult for a book to be overlooked or lost, it provides a record of messages sent home and it allows parents to write a message back to the teacher if they so wish. However, some parents are reluctant to write notes back to the teacher because they do not want to expose their weaknesses in spelling or grammar. Others may think that they have little of value to write back to the teacher about. So teachers should accept that although they encourage all parents to reply to their comments in home–school diaries, parents will vary in their use of this opportunity. Simply because parents do not write in the diary does not mean that they don't value it, which the vast majority of them do.

In special schools and units for children with special needs home–school diaries are typically sent home daily with each child, but this is not always the case and in some schools they are sent home at the end of the week, while in others they are only used for selected pupils. Therefore, there is no reason why home–school diaries should not be used for children with special needs who have been integrated into mainstream classes, even if the child is the only one with such a book.

The home–school diary can be used to exchange information with parents on a wide variety of subjects. For example, it can be used to let parents know about children's accomplishments at school. Or, a note can be made of the topics discussed and activities carried out by children at school so that this can be discussed by parents at home. Alternatively, what children have done at home during the evening or the weekend or the holidays can be noted so that the teacher can follow up these topics at school. Similarly, parents can inform teachers about any circumstances at home which may have upset their child, while teachers can let parents know about any misbehaviour which has occurred at school. However, it is best not to communicate essentially sensitive or negative information by means of the diary; this is better done face to face, as mentioned earlier.

Turnbull and Turnbull (1986) suggest that parents should be involved in deciding what information is included in the diary as well as how often it will be sent home and whether parents want to write in it. In my experience, when parents do decide to write in the diary this method of communication generally works very well and makes a significant contribution to strengthening relationships between the parents and teachers concerned.

A variation on the home–school book, recently suggested by Sicley (1993), is the *Weekly Folder*. This is simply a manilla folder with a sheet of paper with a line down the middle stapled inside it. At the end of the week the teacher writes a brief message for parents on the left-hand side of the sheet and encloses in the folder notices, newsletters, details of homework or samples of the pupils' work for their parents to see. When the folder is taken home parents then have the opportunity to write a comment on the sheet next to the teacher's message. When the sheets get filled up new ones are stapled on top of the old ones so that a record of the messages can be kept. In this way, the Weekly Folder provides a quick and efficient method for maintaining contact with parents and keeping them in touch with what their children are doing at school.

Progress reports

Reports on children's progress are the most longstanding and widely used form of written communication to parents. However, such reports have been undergoing some changes in recent years. A type of report which has become very popular with schools is the *Record of Achievement* (ROA). Although each school develops its own format, ROAs have several common components. First, they list the major achievements made by the pupil in each subject area. Second, pupils comment on these achievements and on their satisfaction with their progress in each subject and on any specific weaknesses they have. Third, pupils state their immediate goals in each subject. Fourth, teachers comment on pupils' achievements and on their immediate goals. Then ROAs are sent out to parents. This is done once a year in most schools but twice or three times a year in some.

However, many parents have been frustrated by the tremendous amount of detail in ROAs and the absence of information which would enable them to compare their children's progress with that of other children of their age. It is perhaps because of parents' dissatisfaction with some aspects of ROAs that statutory guidance on progress reports was published (DFE, 1993). This guidance requires schools to:

- report to parents on their children's progress at least annually;
- report on progress in all subjects and activities at school;
- report on overall progress and on attendance;
- report how the results of assessments on National Curriculum subjects compare with the results of other children of the same age in the school.

PARENT–TEACHER MEETINGS

The form of contact with parents with which all teachers are familiar is that of *parents' evenings* or *parent–teacher interviews*. These meetings are a well-established method of involving parents – and not without reason, as research has shown that they have an impact on both parent–teacher relationships and pupil progress (Turnbull and Turnbull, 1986). It has been found that children whose parents attend such meetings have higher attendance rates, fewer behaviour problems and improved academic achievement. Of course experienced teachers would immediately suggest that this is because the parents of 'good kids' usually attend parents' evenings whereas parents of pupils with behavioural or learning difficulties tend not to turn up. However, as noted in Chapter 2, it must not be assumed that parents who do not turn up to parents' evenings are not interested in their children's education. There is a variety of reasons why some parents do not attend such meetings, including transport and baby-sitting problems, as well as parents' negative feelings about their own school days. Perhaps if these problems could be overcome then these parents would come to parents' evenings and this would lead to better parent–teacher relationships and thereby an improvement in their children's behaviour and progress at school. I believe that it would, but it is usually easier to use other strategies to communicate with these parents than overcome the problems. By using either home visits, telephone contacts or written communication, good parent–teacher relationships can be established which should lead to improvements in children's behaviour and academic progress.

However, it is typically only a minority of parents who don't come to parents' evenings. Regular parent–teacher meetings are desired by the majority of parents, as was noted earlier. The fact that nearly all schools hold such meetings suggests that teachers also find that they are a useful way of communicating between home and school. Bastiani (1989) has suggested that teachers and parents have different goals for such meetings.

Teachers' goals include:

- informing parents of their children's progress;
- establishing good relationships with parents;
- telling parents about the difficulties their children have at school;
- checking with parents how their children are coping with school;
- learning more about children, from parents' perspectives;
- finding out parents' opinions about the school programme;
- identifying ways in which parents can help their children at home;
- identifying potential conflicts between parents and teachers;
- jointly making decisions about children's education.

Parents' goals include:

- meeting all the people who teach their children;
- finding out about their children's progress;
- finding out about any difficulties they are having;
- passing on important information about their children;
- questioning teachers about any concerns they have;
- finding out ways of helping their children at home;
- comparing their child's progress with that of others in the class;
- discussing any difficulties which they are experiencing at home;
- learning more about the school and the methods of teaching used.

Swap (1993) has suggested that an important hidden agenda which parents have at such meetings is to check whether the teacher really knows and understands their child.

Whatever goals teachers and parents have for these meetings, it is important to both participants that they are organized to ensure effective communication. Several authors have provided suggestions for optimizing the effectiveness of parent–teacher meetings (Kroth, 1985; Simpson, 1996; Swap, 1993; Turnbull and Turnbull, 1986). It is from these that the following guidelines are drawn. The guidelines are divided into three sections focusing on tasks for before and after meetings and those for actually conducting meetings.

Organizing parent–teacher meetings

On parents' evenings, because of the typically large number of parents each teacher has to meet with, there is considerable time pressure on parent–teacher interviews. It is therefore important to do as much as possible beforehand to ensure that time in the meeting is used as effectively as possible. The following guidelines are suggested with this aim in mind. They will also apply to additional individual parent–teacher interviews which are set up at the request of either parents or teachers.

Making initial contacts
It is of course preferable if the teacher's first contact with parents is not in a formal parent–teacher interview. It is far better if the initial contact is made by means of a home visit or one of the informal forms of contact discussed earlier. However, this is not always possible, so for many parents this formal situation will be their first contact with their child's teacher.

Notifying parents
Notifying parents about parent–teacher meetings is usually best done by letters of invitation sent home at least two weeks in advance, if possible followed up by less formal reminders two or three days beforehand. Reminders can be a brief note in a child's school bag or a short telephone call. Invitations need to specify the place, time and length of time allotted for the meeting. The purpose of the meeting should be made quite clear and non-threatening so that parents do not worry unnecessarily.

Helping parents prepare
Along with the invitation parents can be sent some guidelines to help them prepare for the meeting. Kroth (1985) suggests that most parents appreciate this because it conveys a message that parental input is welcome at the meeting. Guidelines for parents could include:

- making a list of questions to ask or concerns to raise, e.g. about the child's progress in various subjects, behaviour in class and in the playground, relationships with teachers and other children;
- being prepared to ask for clarification of any unfamiliar terminology which the teacher uses;
- being prepared to comment on children's activities at home, e.g. hobbies, interests and amount of TV watched;
- being prepared to comment on the way children are disciplined at home and what limits are set, e.g. regarding TV viewing, homework completion and bedtime;
- being prepared to comment on factors which may affect children's learning, e.g. child's health, health of other family members, any other relevant family circumstances;
- talking to children to check whether they have any concerns about school or questions they would like the teacher to be asked.

Preparing room
Since physical environment has an impact on the quality of communication in meetings, it is important to book the most suitable venue available. Typically the teacher's classroom will be used and this need not be inappropriate as long as certain basic steps are taken. For example, the most comfortable chairs available should be found and arranged so that there are no physical barriers such as a desk between parents and the teacher. Also, distractions should be

avoided and privacy maintained by keeping the classroom door closed and having a 'Do Not Disturb' sign on the outside of it.

Reviewing children's work
Before the meeting it is useful to review children's records, assessment data and work done at school. Typical examples of children's work can be selected in order to show parents at the meeting.

Involving other staff
Where relevant it is also important to talk with other members of staff who work with the children in order to obtain more information and get their views on the children's progress.

Involving children
Where appropriate, children can be involved in the meeting along with their parents. If this is not considered appropriate then the child should be told about the purpose of the meeting and given the opportunity to have input into the agenda.

Preparing agenda
A list of issues needing to be raised with parents should be made and these should be ranked in order of priority so that key concerns can be dealt with first. It may not be possible to cover all of the issues, since parents are likely to want time to discuss items of concern to them.

Conducting parent–teacher meetings

Although the focus of meetings is necessarily on the issues to be discussed, it must not be forgotten that establishing effective working relationships with parents is more important in the long term. So the manner in which meetings are conducted is of vital importance. It has been suggested that, in the past, parent–teacher meetings have been characterized by a one-way flow of information, from teacher to parent (Simpson, 1996). However, as noted earlier, relationships between parents and teachers can only be successful if there is a two-way communication process which involves sharing information, concerns and ideas (Chinn *et al.*, 1978). Therefore, in order to conduct effective meetings with parents, teachers need to use many of the interpersonal skills which are discussed in Chapter 5, plus those which are referred to below.

Rapport building
When parents first arrive, time should be spent welcoming them and making them feel at ease. They should be thanked for coming and encouraged to ask questions or comment at any time during the meeting.

Structuring
It is always wise to remind parents of the time limits set for the meeting, since

there is good evidence that setting time limits helps to reduce irrelevant discussions (Simpson, 1996). Then the purpose of the meeting can be stated and the agenda items proposed by the teacher can be listed. Parents should be asked if there are other issues or concerns they would like to discuss at the meeting. Parents' items can then be added to the agenda which should be dealt with in agreed priority order.

Note-taking
It is easier to build rapport in a meeting if notes are not taken during it. However, teachers often find it useful to note important details and list things they need to do after the meeting. Parents may also want to make notes. So the issue of note-taking should be discussed at the beginning of the meeting. If teachers explain the reasons for wanting to take notes, are sensitive about what they write down and allow parents to see what they have written, then this should not interfere with the communication process.

Providing information
It is usually best to start on a positive note by stating the areas in which the child is doing well. Concerns the teacher has about difficulties the child is experiencing or creating should be stated clearly and specifically but with sensitivity. Parents want teachers to be honest with them but not brutal. If part of the difficulty which teachers need to convey involves providing some negative feedback to parents, for example if pupils are consistently not doing their homework and parents do not appear to be monitoring this, then the modified DESC script (see Chapter 5) can be used.

Obtaining information
In order to get parents to open up and share concerns and ideas, teachers need to use the skills of attentiveness, asking open-ended questions, paraphrasing and active listening which are discussed in Chapter 5.

Problem-solving
Where specific problems emerge with no obvious solutions or where teachers and parents disagree, then the problem-solving procedure, which is discussed in Chapter 5, should be used.

Termination
At the end of the meeting teachers should summarize the main points which have emerged and review the action which both parents and teachers have agreed to take. If more time is needed, then further meetings should be arranged. Finally, parents should be thanked for their participation and reminded that they can contact the teacher any time they require information or have a concern about their child.

Reviewing parent–teacher meetings

Following the meeting teachers have several tasks to complete in order to make best use of the outcome of the meeting.

Making a record
A brief report should be written to summarize the main issues which were discussed and the decisions which emerged from the meeting. It should record the individuals responsible for carrying out each recommendation which was agreed upon.

Discussing with children
A brief review of the items discussed at the meeting should be conducted with the children involved and the impact of any recommendations on them explained. Children should then be given the opportunity to ask questions about the meeting.

Liaising with colleagues
Other members of staff should be informed about the outcome of the meeting and any recommendations relevant to their work with the child discussed with them.

Planning for follow-up
Teachers need to plan for the implementation of the recommendations agreed at the meeting and for any follow-up meetings which were scheduled.

Evaluating
The best way for teachers to get feedback from parents on the effectiveness of the meetings from their perspective is to ask parents to complete a brief questionnaire. Several writers have provided sample questionnaires (see Kroth, 1985; Simpson, 1996; Turnbull and Turnbull, 1986) in which parents are asked to rate aspects of the parent–teacher meeting such as: the suitability of the room used; the adequacy of the time available; the appropriateness of the agenda; the adequacy of information obtained; the quality of the teacher's listening skills; the helpfulness of recommendations.

HOME VISITS

Many parents appreciate it when their children's teachers are prepared to come and visit them on their own territory. Such home visits can be pivotal in establishing close working relationships with parents. They enable teachers to see for themselves the circumstances in which the family are living. They also enable teachers to meet other members of the family such as siblings and fathers whom they may not otherwise meet. Knowledge of these factors can help teachers understand how their pupils may be affected by the home situation.

Home visits also enable teachers to find out how their pupils spend their time at home, whether they have any hobbies, how much television they watch and what time they usually go to bed. It is also possible to find out how pupils behave at home and how their parents handle them. Finally, home visits provide an opportunity for teachers to answer parents' questions and deal with any concerns they may have.

However, not all parents want home visits, as reported in the survey noted earlier. Some parents may be too embarrassed to allow teachers to see their homes, others may fear what neighbours may say about a teacher's visit. As also shown by the surveys, more parents appreciate home visits than actually get them. This is because most teachers do not see home visits as a high priority. The reasons for the low priority given to home visiting by teachers are hard to assess. It is possible that teachers are generally not aware of how much many parents appreciate receiving home visits from their children's teachers. Also, teachers may not realize the benefits which can accrue for them and their pupils from making such home visits. There are also difficulties for teachers with families themselves in making home visits, since in most cases this would need to be done in the evening because they are teaching all day. In recognition of this problem and the value to children of improving relationships between school and home, some English LEAs in the late 1980s set up 'Home–School Liaison Schemes'. The scheme in Humberside involved selected primary schools having a teacher, half of whose time was used to release class teachers during the school day so that they could make home visits to the parents of children whose progress or behaviour was causing a concern.

In contrast, many secondary schools still actively discourage classroom teachers from having contacts with parents other than on parents' evenings. But this is certainly not true of them all. For example, one secondary school in a socially deprived area of Hull is well known for ensuring that visits are made each year to the homes of all their new intake of pupils before they begin. The visits are made by the teachers and senior teachers who will be involved with the new intake of pupils and are considered to have significantly reduced the level of behavioural problems at the school.

Guidelines for home visits

In order to optimize the effectiveness of home visits, some general guidelines should be followed. These are outlined below.

Arranging visits

Home visits should always be pre-arranged since some parents would be embarrassed about the tidiness and cleanliness of their house if teachers just arrived unannounced. It is usually best for teachers to write letters to parents saying that they wish to make home visits to the parents of all their pupils and will be phoning in the next few days to make arrangements with those parents who would like this.

Dress
Since in their own homes parents will be dressed casually, it is best if teachers dress less formally than they do at school so that parents will feel more at ease. Some parents may find it more difficult to open up with a teacher dressed in a suit and tie when they are dressed casually.

Time
It is clearly best to arrange to visit at a time of day when all the family members will be present and when parents will have a chance to talk. For most families, the middle of the evening, when they have finished their evening meal, is the best time. It is important to be punctual and to allow sufficient time for the visit. It is also important not to stay too long as parents will need time to get the children ready for bed and possibly do other chores ready for the morning. It is usually best to allow for visits to last between one and two hours but to set a limit half an hour before your actual deadline to cope with the phenomenon that parents will mention their greatest concern just as you are leaving!

Courtesy
It is important to respect the hospitality associated with the cultural group from which the family comes. With most English families this will simply mean accepting the offer of a cup of tea or coffee, but for West Indian families it will probably mean accepting something to eat as well. When I was teaching in New Zealand and made a home visit to a Samoan family I found that they had prepared a full meal of Samoan food all served on banana leaves for my arrival. Fortunately, I had been forewarned that it is not possible to discuss important matters in a Samoan household until you have eaten with the family!

Listening
Throughout the visit teachers need to be aware of using the listening skills discussed in Chapter 5 in order to help parents express their priorities and concerns about their children.

Questions
Teachers will want to ask parents for information about their children such as about any medical problems or about their behaviour at home. It is also important to give parents time to ask questions of the teacher.

Distractions
Teachers should anticipate that there are likely to be distractions during the visit and be determined not to become irritated by them.

SUMMARY AND CONCLUSIONS

A range of possible strategies for communicating with parents has been discussed in this chapter. Informal contacts such as open days, school productions and outings were suggested as ways of 'breaking the ice'. Several forms of written communication were considered including handbooks, newsletters, progress reports and home–school diaries. Guidelines were also provided for the use of telephone contacts with parents, and the organization, conduct and review of parent–teacher meetings was discussed at length. Finally, the importance of home visits in building relationships with parents was stressed and guidelines for making them were provided. In conclusion, it can be seen that a wide variety of strategies is available to teachers for communicating with parents. The actual methods used will depend on teacher and parent preferences, but in general it is considered that making a range of strategies available to parents will lead to substantial improvements in the level of parental involvement in schools.

Chapter 4

Parental Involvement in their Children's Education

During my two years working in Barbados I was asked to lead several workshops for parents of children with special needs in mainstream schools. The focus of the workshops was to be on what parents could do to help their children at home. At some point during most of these workshops parents would ask how they could help their children to read if they couldn't read too well themselves. My reply was that this need not be a reason for not helping. In order to explain why, I described an important piece of research carried out a few years ago which involved five children and their mothers, who had recently arrived in New Zealand from Cambodia (Glynn and Glynn, 1986). None of the mothers could either read or speak more than a few words of English before the study. They were taught how to use a shared reading procedure (described later in this chapter) in order to help their children learn to read. The mothers engaged in shared reading sessions with their children every night after school. This was in addition to the school reading programme which the children were following and to small-group tuition from the English-as-a-Second-Language teacher.

The results of the study showed that, over a period of just 24 weeks, the children made gains of from one to two years in their reading attainment. From the research design used it was possible to see that the most dramatic gains in reading ability were made when the shared reading was begun. This result was even more startling because the parents involved were themselves learning to read English along with their children.

The findings of this study provide very strong support for the effectiveness of parental involvement in their children's education because, if parents who can hardly speak English can facilitate their children's reading progress through working with them at home, parents who have literacy difficulties themselves should also be able to help. In fact, the potential benefits for all parents to help in this way are clear.

This chapter will discuss a variety of approaches to involving parents in the education of their children. The approaches will be considered in approximate chronological order of their development. The first types of parental involvement grew out of the early intervention schemes of the 1960s and 1970s. At about the same time the training of parents in techniques to modify their children's behaviour began to be developed. The 1980s saw the rapid development of schemes designed to involve parents in helping their children to read. These were followed by schemes which focused on other curriculum areas such as mathematics and spelling. Finally, in the last decade, there has been an increasing impetus to improve the involvement of parents in the assessment of their children and in reviews of their progress.

EARLY INTERVENTION PROJECTS

Early intervention for disadvantaged pre-school children in the USA began in the 1960s under the Headstart project, which was a key element in President Kennedy's 'war on poverty'. A variety of schemes was established in different parts of the country, each with its own approach. The majority of these programmes were centre-based, with parents typically bringing along their children for a few half-day sessions each week. Programmes varied in the extent to which they involved parents, with some having only minimal involvement.

Initial evaluations of the effectiveness of the schemes suggested that large gains in IQ could be achieved. However, follow-up studies found that the IQ gains had generally disappeared after two years of primary schooling, so the focus was placed on maintenance of the early gains. Bronfenbrenner's (1976) analysis of the research evidence suggested that the programmes which had higher levels of parent involvement were the ones which produced higher levels of immediate gains and that these gains were more likely to be maintained as children progressed through primary school. Teacher–parent contacts in general and home visits in particular seemed to be associated with more effective programmes. This finding led to increased attention being paid to early intervention projects which were home-based, such as the Portage Project which is discussed later in this section.

Follow-up studies have shown that early intervention programmes have important long-term effects, as noted earlier (Berrueta-Clement *et al.*, 1984). It has been estimated that seven dollars are saved for every dollar spent on early intervention because of reductions in such things as remedial teaching, special education placements, payment of unemployment benefits, and costs to the criminal justice system. This powerful argument in favour of early intervention and parent involvement has been used to support the idea of expanding nursery provision in the UK so that it is available to all pre-school children.

Project High/Scope

One of the programmes which has recently been gaining popularity in the UK is Project High/Scope. This programme evolved from the Perry Preschool

Project (Berrueta-Clement *et al.*, 1984). The philosophy of High/Scope is based on the work of Piaget and Dewey, so the importance of active learning and children using their initiative is emphasized. The programme has mainly been used with children aged 3 to 5 years and typically involves daily three-hour sessions based at a pre-school centre coupled with weekly home visits. High/Scope has several components which are considered to be essential to its success: child-initiated learning; a structured environment; a daily routine; key experiences; and a high level of parental involvement.

Child-initiated learning occurs because High/Scope teachers provide opportunities for children to learn actively and construct their own knowledge. Children are given control over the learning situation and acquire knowledge by actively experiencing the world around them by choosing, exploring, manipulating and experimenting with the materials provided. The environment is structured so that children have a choice between developmentally appropriate activities which will provide certain key experiences designed to facilitate the development of logical thinking and promote cognitive, social, physical, and emotional development.

A distinctive feature of the programme is the establishment of a daily routine which includes the use of a *plan–do–review* sequence. At the start of each session children are asked to choose the activities they want to engage in and *plan* how they will spend their time. In the *do* phase teachers support, enquire about and extend children's play. At the end of the session children are asked to *review* their day's play either symbolically or verbally in order to link the planning and doing phases.

The role of parents is regarded as being crucial to the effectiveness of the programme. Therefore, parental participation is encouraged in all aspects of High/Scope. In particular, teachers make weekly home visits of about 90 minutes, during which the child's progress is discussed and parents are invited to observe and participate in various activities with their children. Parents are encouraged to see themselves as experts on their children and as partners with teachers in the programme.

Portage Project

During the late 1960s, early intervention programmes began to be established for children with delayed development. The best known of these is the Portage Project which was established in Portage, Wisconsin in 1969 (Shearer and Shearer, 1972). The Portage programme is designed to help parents, and possibly other members of their extended family, to teach their children at home. A major aim of the programme is to develop parents' skills so that they can work with their children in the home. The programme has five components:

1. a checklist of developmental skills;
2. teaching cards;
3. activity charts;

4. a book of readings;
5. home visits from a Portage worker.

The Portage checklist consists of 580 items divided into six colour-coded areas of development:

1. cognitive skills;
2. language skills;
3. social skills;
4. fine and gross motor skills;
5. activities of daily living;
6. a section on infant stimulation.

In each area the items are ordered in approximate developmental sequence for children from birth to 6 years. The checklist is initially used by the Portage worker to assess the child in each of the six areas of development. Through a combination of discussion with the parents and observation of the child, the items on the checklist which the child has already accomplished are ticked off. The checklist items just beyond those ticked then provide ideas for aspects of the child's development which should be taught next.

The teaching cards each have a checklist item written as a behavioural objective, along with suggestions of how to teach this skill. The cards are sequenced and colour-coded the same as the checklist so that parents can easily find the card corresponding to the checklist item they are going to teach.

The activity cards are for recording the teaching activities which parents work on between visits from the Portage worker. The book of readings provides parents with a description of and a rationale for the teaching system used in the Portage programme.

Home visits by the Portage worker are normally weekly and are scheduled to last about 1½ hours. The child's progress on the item which parents have worked on over the week is checked by referring to the activity card and by getting the child to demonstrate the skill. If the child can now accomplish this task a tick is placed on the checklist and another item is selected to work on. If the child has not yet learned the particular skill, the Portage worker will discuss alternative teaching strategies with the parents.

The emphasis in the programme is on Portage workers establishing partnerships with parents, with the aim of empowering them to facilitate the development of their children. Thus, the concept of professionals sharing their skills with parents is a key element of the programme. In practice, Portage workers find that allowing time on home visits for discussing parents' concerns about their children helps to promote this partnership. In various adapted forms the Portage model is now widely used in the UK (White and Cameron, 1988) and in over 30 countries throughout the world (Brouillette *et al.*, 1993).

HOME–SCHOOL BEHAVIOUR PROGRAMMES

The benefits of home–school behaviour programmes were made clear to me when, as a trainee educational psychologist, I was asked to deal with a 12-year-old girl who was on the point of being excluded from school. Carol was disruptive in class, argued openly with teachers and used offensive language as well as frequently having disputes with other pupils in class and in the playground. The most obvious intervention was a behaviour modification programme, designed in collaboration with her teachers, which would be instituted throughout the school day. However, Carol's teachers said that they had tried behaviour modification programmes to no avail, and were not willing to consider rewards or incentives for Carol over and above those available to other pupils in the school.

A solution to this problem was found by using what have come to be known as 'home–school behaviour programmes' or 'school–home notes' (Atkeson and Forehand, 1979; Kelley, 1990). This approach is based on the idea that collaboration between teachers and parents is the most effective way to solve children's behaviour problems. It requires teachers to specify the changes in behaviour which are needed and then to monitor the pupil's behaviour on a specially designed report form. The parents' role is to provide rewards for the child when the pre-set target on the report form is achieved.

In this case Carol's teachers were interviewed in order to determine which of her behaviours were most disruptive and needed to be changed. A list of appropriate alternative behaviours was then placed on the specially designed report form (see Figure 4.1). Finishing the academic tasks she had been set was one of the criteria listed on Carol's incentive programme, but the major focus was on her behaviour. Carol's teachers simply recorded the appropriateness of her behaviour on the report form at the end of each lesson. When she took the report form home at the end of the week, Carol's parents provided certain incentives, which had been agreed with Carol, depending on the details of the teachers' report on her behaviour over the week. The incentives included staying up half an hour later at night, visiting her grandmother, and going swimming.

From the day this programme started, Carol's behaviour improved dramatically and she presented no further problems of any significance for the remainder of the school year. The key to this positive outcome was involving Carol's parents in a positive way. In the past, contacts between home and school had consisted mainly of teachers informing the parents about her misdemeanours. Once the programme started teachers were reporting mostly appropriate behaviour so Carol's parents were put in the position of rewarding her for good behaviour rather than being expected to punish her for the misdemeanours she had committed. Hence, this form of parental involvement consisted mainly of a structure which enabled Carol's parents to provide support to her teachers in ensuring that she behaved appropriately at school.

CAROL ————————   **INCENTIVE PROGRAMME**

Week ending:_____

To be completed by class teacher at the end of each school day and sent home with Carol on Friday.

Behaviour	Mon. a.m. p.m.	Tues. a.m. p.m.	Wed. a.m. p.m.	Thurs. a.m. p.m.	Fri. a.m. p.m.
1. Starting work quietly without reminder.					
2. Not letting other pupils disturb her.					
3. Finishing work set.					
4. Remaining at desk.					
5. Using a quiet voice in class.					
6. Using appropriate language.					
7. Respecting teacher's decisions.					
8. Leaving classroom quietly.					
9. Mature behaviour at interval.					
10. Not fiddling with clothing.					
TOTALS					

GRAND TOTAL FOR WEEK: _____

5 points: acceptable behaviour   3 points: 1 slip up
1 point: 2 slip-ups   0 points: more than 2 slip-ups

[____] points and over: Carol allowed up half an hour later at night (9 p.m.)

[____] points and over: Carol allowed to go swimming or visit Nana

COMMENTS:

Signed:
(Class teacher)

Figure 4.1: Home–school report form

PARENT BEHAVIOURAL TRAINING

The most radical approach to parental involvement in education has gained steadily in popularity since it emerged during the 1970s (Berkowitz and Graziano, 1972; Graziano and Diament, 1992). The aim of parent behavioural training (PBT) is to teach parents the skills of behaviour modification so that they can work directly on their children's behaviour problems or learning difficulties. The idea is that parents act as their children's behaviour therapists or teachers, either alone or in collaboration with professionals.

There are several components of the rationale for this approach. First, it is considered that parents are children's natural teachers since they teach them self-help and language skills in the pre-school years. Second, since parents spend so much time with their children they have ample opportunities for teaching them. Third, involving parents in this way should result in long-term gains for their children since parents will have learned skills they can use throughout childhood. Fourth, training parents to act as therapists or teachers to their children, rather than professionals working with them directly, is more cost-effective in terms of professional time.

In the first years of PBT the emphasis was very much on remediating children's behaviour problems, but subsequently children's learning difficulties have received more attention. For example, parents have been trained to act as therapists for children with delayed language (Topping, 1986). Also, the technology of PBT has progressed substantially since the early days. At first, PBT programmes relied solely on teaching parents how to positively reinforce appropriate behaviour. Then, when it was realized that this had limited effectiveness, the technique of extinction, or ignoring inappropriate behaviour, was added. Later, it was realized that successful training needed to include teaching parents effective methods of punishment such as withdrawal of privileges and time out. As sophistication in the techniques taught to parents for dealing with behaviour problems increased, so did those for remediating learning difficulties. In addition, the methods used to train parents in these techniques became increasingly sophisticated. These aspects of PBT are discussed in detail in Topping (1986) and the main components are summarized below.

Training methods

The methods used to train parents in behavioural principles and techniques have included:

- lecture presentations;
- video-taped modelling;
- live modelling;
- role play;
- behavioural rehearsal;
- feedback;
- home visits;
- telephone monitoring of progress;
- parent self-recording;
- parent training manuals.

Of the wide range of training methods noted above which have been used, Graziano and Diament (1992) found that self-instructional materials, such as the parent training manuals written by Patterson (1975) and Newsome and Hipgrave (1982), could be successful and cost-cffcctive. However, the most effective forms of PBT were found to be ones which included the active participation of parents, such as modelling and role play, or feedback given on home visits.

Training content

The techniques taught to parents to deal with their children's behaviour problems have included:

- observation techniques;
- methods of parent recording;
- contingent attention (positive reinforcement);
- point incentive systems (star charts and token systems);
- extinction (ignoring);
- time out (isolation);
- response cost (withdrawal of privileges);
- contingency contracting (for secondary school-age children);
- fading (of extrinsic reinforcers back to natural consequences).

The techniques taught to parents in order that they can remediate their children's learning difficulties include:

- the effective use of rewards;
- prompting;
- cueing;
- task analysis;
- shaping;
- backward chaining;
- fading.

Graziano and Diament (1992) conclude from their recent review that PBT has been found to be effective in dealing with a wide range of children's behaviour problems and learning difficulties. Parents have been shown to benefit from PBT by improving their knowledge of behavioural techniques and application of child management skills, as well as in developing more positive attitudes to their children. Individual and group PBT were found to be equally effective, which suggests that since group PBT is more cost-effective, this may generally be the preferred approach. Group behavioural training is discussed in Chapter 6.

PARENTAL INVOLVEMENT IN READING

A type of parental involvement in the education of children in mainstream primary and secondary schools which has gained considerably in popularity since the late 1970s involves parents helping their children with reading at home. Parent involvement with reading has taken a variety of forms, based on the different approaches or programmes which have been adopted by schools, as documented in Topping and Wolfendale (1985). Three of the most widely used types of programmes for promoting parental involvement in reading are parent listening, paired reading and the approach known as Pause, Prompt and Praise. These three approaches are outlined below.

Parent listening to children read

Listening to children read the books they bring home from school is the time-honoured way for parents to help their children learn to read. It is a method now used in virtually all primary schools in one way or another. The effectiveness of this approach was affirmed by the study conducted by Tizard *et al.* (1982) which was referred to earlier in this book. The results of this study showed that when parents listened to their children read at home they made substantial gains in reading attainment. Furthermore, these gains were greater than those made by other children who had been given extra tuition in reading at school instead of being exposed to parent listening. In addition, a follow-up study has subsequently found that the gains which children in the parent listening group had made were maintained four years later (Hewison, 1985).

Another study which focused on parent listening was conducted in Belfield, a low SES suburb of Rochdale, about a mile from where I grew up (Hannon *et al.*, 1985). The aim of the project was to encourage as many parents as possible to hear their children read on a regular basis. Parents enrolled in the project when their children were aged 5 years and many participated for two or three years. Meetings held at the school were used to explain the project to the parents. Later in the project these meetings included an introductory video. Carefully designed procedures were implemented to ensure that parents listened to their children read each night after school. Plastic folders were supplied so that books could be safely transported to and from school by the children. Record cards which parents filled in were used so that teachers could monitor parent listening and quickly identify any parents who needed help.

Considerable emphasis was placed on maintaining close working relationships with parents throughout their involvement in the project. Parents were all visited at home at least once during the first term that they became involved in the project. Meetings were held at school about the project, at which lists of what to do and what not to do were handed out. In addition, letters were regularly sent home with the children and teachers attempted to speak to parents at every opportunity, such as when they were dropping off their children at school or picking them up. In fact, it was considered that a key factor in maintaining parents' interest in and co-operation with the project was the personal relationships which teachers established with parents.

Before the project began 38 per cent of parents reported that they listened to their children read almost daily. The mean reading quotient of the children whose parents listened to them read was found to be significantly higher than that of the remaining children, as found in other studies of parent listening. Interviews carried out with parents who had spent two years in the project found that 90 per cent of children were heard reading almost daily at home. This represents a substantial improvement in the level of parent involvement in their children's reading which, surprisingly, did not result in a significant improvement in overall levels of achievement in reading for the children involved (Hannon, 1987). However, it is possible that the project had a long-term impact on these children's progress due to raising their parents' awareness of the value of involving themselves in their children's education.

The two studies of parent listening described above provide a powerful rationale for the use of such schemes. One of the main advantages of this approach is its versatility. Parent listening can be used to support any approach to reading or reading scheme which schools use. Also, it requires minimal input of teacher time and other resources for what is an appreciable benefit. The main weakness of this approach is the uncertainty about 'how' parents listen to their children reading. What do they actually do? It is very likely that different parents will handle the sessions quite differently, and it is possible that some parents may create problems through their lack of understanding of how children learn to read. For this reason the technique of 'paired reading', which is described in the next section, is generally regarded as a superior approach.

Paired reading

The main way in which paired reading differs from parent listening is that more guidance is provided on how parents should act when they are hearing children read. Parents are encouraged to use the procedure regularly for short periods. Children are allowed to select their own books for reading to their parents. The paired reading procedure has two phases. In the first phase the parent and child read together out loud, with the parent adjusting to the child's pace of reading. When the child reads a word incorrectly the parent says the word correctly and gets the child to repeat the word before the two of them continue reading together.

In the second phase, when children feel confident enough to read alone, they signal to the parent to be silent, usually by a nudge from the elbow, and continue to read aloud by themselves. The parent then praises the child for taking this initiative and continues to praise the child's efforts when difficult words are mastered and when errors are spontaneously corrected by the child. When the child makes a mistake the parent says the word correctly, gets the child to repeat the word and then joins in reading out loud with the child as before. When the child gets stuck on a word the parent waits about four or five seconds and then supplies the word and gets the child to say it correctly before continuing to read aloud together. When children again feel confident they can once more signal to the parent to be silent and continue to read on by themselves.

Several variations of the paired reading procedure are reported in Topping and Wolfendale (1985). One variation is 'shared reading' which is regarded to be a simplification of paired reading (Greening and Spenceley, 1984). Shared reading simply involves parents reading aloud with their children while ignoring any mistakes that they make. The aim of this approach is to increase the flow of reading and focus attention onto the meaning of the text. In another variation an additional phase is added to the paired reading procedure to cope with books of high interest to children but which are really too difficult for them. The first phase consists of parents reading a short passage aloud by themselves with children following the text. The second phase involves the parent and child reading the passage aloud together, with parents either correcting mistakes or supplying words as described above. In the third phase children attempt to read the passage by themselves with parents correcting and praising as above (Bryans *et al.*, 1985).

In all paired reading approaches the key factors in ensuring effectiveness are how well parents are trained to carry out the procedures and the monitoring and support provided to ensure that parents correctly implement the procedures at home. Most paired reading projects begin by organizing a meeting of interested parents at school. This meeting is often also used to provide group training to parents in operating the procedures. Many LEAs have demonstration videotapes of the paired reading procedures available for schools to borrow to show parents. Alternatively, in some projects parents have been given brief individual training in carrying out paired reading (Bryans *et al.*, 1985). Record sheets for parents to fill in after each reading session are also used to provide a means of monitoring how parents and children are getting on.

Reviews of studies which have compared the effectiveness of parent listening, paired reading and other procedures in improving children's reading attainment have suggested that paired reading is generally the most effective approach (Topping, 1985; Topping and Lindsay, 1992). A recent study has found that a key element in the effectiveness of paired reading is that parents are able to maintain the flow of reading so that children's interest in and comprehension of what they are reading is enhanced (Elliott and Hewison, 1994). It is suggested that paired reading helps to shift the emphasis away from viewing reading as an exercise to be worked through to focusing on comprehension and enjoyment of the story.

However, Elliott and Hewison also reported that many parents complained that using this approach all the time was too limiting. They wanted to use additional strategies to help their children cope with words they found difficult. This is precisely the aim of the approach known as Pause, Prompt and Praise, which is described in the next section.

Pause, Prompt and Praise

The approach to parental involvement in reading called Pause, Prompt and Praise (PPP) was developed in New Zealand by Glynn (1985) and his colleagues. The emphasis in the PPP approach is on careful training of parents in a tutoring procedure which focuses on the meaning of the text and emphasizes the need to allow children time to 'self-correct' any errors they make. The PPP tutoring procedure includes the following aspects. First of all, it is important to ensure that children are given reading material of an appropriate level of difficulty; that is text on which their reading accuracy is between 80 and 95 per cent. Below 80 per cent accuracy the material is too difficult, 95 per cent and above it is too easy. Therefore, parents are taught a simple way of checking difficulty level so that books of a suitable level can be selected for tutoring. Most often the PPP approach is used in conjunction with a reading scheme which includes a series of books graded into progressive difficulty levels. This facilitates the selection of books for parents and children to work on.

In the first step of the PPP tutoring procedure, when children make an error, parents pause for a few seconds to allow children to attempt to correct it themselves. If this does not happen then parents offer prompts related to the type of error that is made. If the mistake does not make sense then the parent prompts with clues about the meaning of the story. If the mistake does make sense then the parent prompts with clues about how the word looks. When children do not attempt to say the word then they are told to read on to the end of the sentence, or to re-read the sentence from the beginning, in order to help them focus on contextual clues. If the incorrect word is not read correctly after two prompts, the word is supplied. Praise is given for correct reading, self-correction and for correcting mistakes following prompts.

The research studies on PPP have typically involved individual training of parent tutors with twice-weekly sessions held in their homes (Glynn, 1985). Parents were given a diagrammatic summary of the PPP procedure, and feedback was provided on actual tutoring sessions which they were observed conducting with their children and on other tutoring sessions which they recorded on audio tapes. In studies carried out in both Auckland and Birmingham very promising results were obtained with children whose attainments in reading were markedly delayed.

A booklet for parents explaining the procedure has been produced (Glynn *et al.*, 1979) and subsequently a trainer's manual and videotape demonstration of PPP have become available (McNaughton *et al.*, 1987). So it is now possible to set up projects using PPP involving less intensive methods such as group training of parent tutors, in the same way that this is done in paired reading and parent listening projects. In fact, Merrett (1988), in his review of the literature on the topic, suggests that parents can be taught the PPP procedures 'relatively quickly and easily and that their application is successful in bringing about important changes for the better in low-progress readers' (p. 22).

PARENTAL INVOLVEMENT IN OTHER CURRICULUM AREAS

Following the success of projects aimed at increasing parental involvement in reading, this general approach has also begun to be focused on other areas of the school curriculum, from basic academic skills such as spelling to more specific aspects such as European awareness. Topping (1986) describes parent involvement programmes which have focused on perceptual training for nursery age children, spelling for primary school children and mathematics for secondary school children. Wolfendale (1992) outlines projects which have focused on language development, literacy skills and numeracy. Excellent examples of programmes which have focused on curriculum areas other than reading are the M.A.T.H.S. projects co-ordinated by Bamford and Arora (1988) and a spelling programme conducted by Pilgrim (1999).

Home–school maths programme

Bamford and Arora describe a series of projects aimed at involving parents in helping their children with mathematics using a games approach. All the projects were aimed at children in primary schools and followed a similar format. First, the project co-ordinators, who were educational psychologists, met with the headteacher and members of staff to decide on the children to be involved and the length of the project, which was usually six or eight weeks. Next, parents were invited to a meeting at the school, at which the project was described and a booklet about the project given out. At the end of the meeting parents chose a mathematics game to take home to play with their children. Over 40 different games were used, all focusing on early mathematical concepts such as matching, shape and conservation. Accompanying each game was a card with a list of words to use while playing the game and on which parents recorded the amount of time spent playing the game. It was suggested that parents spend ten to fifteen minutes each day playing the game with their children over the following week. Parents then visited the school each week to exchange their games. At the end of the project parents were invited to the school to discuss their experiences and provide feedback to the organizers. Finally, they were given a booklet of mathematics games to take home.

The authors have attempted to evaluate the projects through feedback from parents and teachers involved and from observations of the children. They conclude that both parents and children enjoy playing the games and that children's confidence and enjoyment of mathematics increases following the project. They also suggest that the projects result in an increase in children's understanding of mathematical language and concepts.

Home–school spelling programme

Pilgrim (1999) conducted a project aimed at involving parents of secondary school pupils in helping their children with spelling. All of the first-year intake of a large comprehensive school were given a spelling test. After the weakest pupils had been selected for specialist assistance from the special needs staff it was clear that there were other pupils whose spelling difficulties, while not severe, did warrant attention. Since these pupils were not to receive extra tuition at school it was decided to set up programmes which parents could work on with their children at home.

Parents of the seventeen pupils who fell into this category were invited to a meeting at the school. The organization of the project was described at the meeting, after which ten parents agreed to be involved, the remaining parents and their children acting as a comparison group. The ten parents were given written guidance on how to help their children with spelling, including using the Look, Cover, Write, Check procedure. Their children were given a series of spelling worksheets graded in levels of difficulty to work through with their parents at home. They were also given notebooks and recording sheets which were used by the special needs staff to monitor their progress. It was suggested to parents that children should achieve 90 per cent success on a worksheet on two consecutive occasions before moving on to the next one. All remaining pupils received no help in spelling other than was part of the normal English curriculum.

All pupils in the first year were retested on the same spelling test eight months later. It was found that the ten pupils in the parent involvement group made, on average, eighteen months' progress in their spelling ages. The group of pupils who were at a similar level but whose parents declined involvement in the project made, on average, eleven months' progress, while the remainder of first-year pupils made an average of nine months' progress. The results of this small-scale study suggest that involving parents did have a significant impact on their children's progress with spelling. Also, since this gain was achieved with only one group meeting of parents and teachers and the supply of worksheets, written guidance and recording sheets, it was a very cost-effective intervention.

FACILITATING PARENTAL INVOLVEMENT IN ASSESSMENTS AND REVIEWS

The importance of involving parents in the assessment of their children and reviews of their progress has recently been reinforced by the emphasis placed on this aspect of parental involvement in the *Code of Practice for Special Educational Needs* (DFE, 1994). Since parental involvement in assessments and reviews, including statutory assessments and annual reviews of statements, are now mandated by the *Code of Practice*, schools will have to think very carefully about how they are going to involve parents who have children with special educational needs. In addition, children with special needs of any kind, including those coping with medical conditions and losses due to bereavement or divorce, also benefit from maximum involvement of their parents in their education. Therefore, facilitating optimum involvement of parents in assessments and reviews is considered important for children with all types of special needs.

In fact, Wolfendale (1992) suggests that assessments should ideally be conducted by means of a partnership between parents and teachers. In the early stages this should encompass the sharing of information, with both parents and teachers setting out their opinions and concerns about children. Later, more specific data on the child's development can be collected by parents and teachers by such means as observations, checklists and tests. The information collected is then shared in a parent–teacher meeting so that an assessment of the child's behaviour and attainments in both home and school settings is achieved. Viewing parental and teacher assessment data as complementary in this way leads to a more open sharing of concerns and ideas between the two and thereby promotes the development of a collaborative partnership.

Assessments: what parents want

Many parents experience considerable anxiety about assessments conducted with their children. They realize the importance of the results of such assessments in making decisions about their children's education. Most parents are therefore very keen to know about any assessments their children are to undergo and like to receive feedback on such assessments as soon as possible afterwards.

Wolfendale (1992) suggests that parents typically have five main expectations when their children are assessed. They:

1. want to know what steps will be taken as a result of the assessment and what they can do to help;
2. want to be able to discuss their children's past performance with their current teacher;
3. want to hear constructive comments on their children's current rate of progress in relation to their previous achievements and to the performance of other children;
4. want to know what strategies teachers are going to use in order to address their children's difficulties;
5. seek confirmation that their children are happy and making progress in their current school.

Broadfoot (1989) reports some research which highlights key aspects of the information about assessments which parents want from teachers. Most importantly, it needs to be *objective*; that is, information must be able to be substantiated rather than merely being based on speculation. Also, it needs to be *constructive*; that is, teachers' comments must include strategies for improving progress. The information must also be *significant*; that is, it should focus on important areas of the child's development. Ideally, the information should also be *succinct*; that is, teachers' comments should be brief and to the point. It also needs to be *goal-related*; that is, comments should be related to parents' goals for their children. Finally, such information must be *broadly based*; that is, it should focus on a broad view of their children's needs.

What parents can contribute to assessments

Wolfendale (1992) has summarized the research on parental contributions to assessments and concluded that '... the quality of content of parental input is equal to that of trained professionals ... ' (p. 79). She considers that parents can make an invaluable contribution to the assessment process for several reasons. First of all, parents have extensive knowledge of their children's development from birth onwards, from which they can contribute comments about any specific difficulties they have experienced or particular assets which they have demonstrated. Parents also have an intimate knowledge of the family history and current circumstances which may be affecting the child. In addition, parents often have knowledge of other factors, related to the wider social environment in which the family lives, which can have an impact on the child. Parents can also supply knowledge of their children's behaviour in the home setting which may well be different from that at school. Furthermore, the information supplied by parents is considered to complement that from professionals and therefore can serve to highlight concerns regarding their children's progress. Finally, it is considered that parents are able to make realistic appraisals of their children and thereby make a significant contribution to the assessment process.

Increasing the effectiveness of parental involvement in assessments and reviews

It has been argued above that involving parents in the assessment and review processes is likely to significantly improve the quality of information available. It is therefore important to attempt to optimize the effectiveness of parental involvement in these processes. In the past, parents were often seen merely as recipients of information who were asked to comment on the assessment data produced by professionals. It is now considered that the effectiveness of assessments and reviews is substantially improved when parents are treated as active partners in the process of collecting and reviewing assessment data. However, most parents are unlikely to contribute optimally unless their involvement is actively sought by teachers. Strategies which can be used to increase parental involvement in assessments and reviews are discussed below.

Assessments: pro-formas for parents
Several examples of strategies used to improve the effectiveness of parental input into the assessment of children have been reported by Wolfendale (1993). These have involved the completion of diaries, observation charts, developmental checklists and parental profiles, by parents, in collaboration with teachers, in order to assess the behaviour and development of children. Parental profiles have been used in situations as diverse as assessing children's progress prior to their entry into school as rising 5-year-olds, and preparing material to present as the parental advice required for statutory assessments of special educational needs.

There is now general recognition of the benefits of providing parents with pro-formas to guide their input into the assessment process. The *Code of Practice* (DFE, 1994) provides guidelines to this effect. It therefore seems expedient to use these for all assessments conducted with children who have special needs. Clearly, different pro-formas will need to be used for children of different ages and to suit the particular situation for which they are to be used. However, most pro-formas will seek information from parents about the following:

- *child's health*, especially any medication taken or known medical problems;
- *gross motor skills*, such as walking, jumping and throwing;
- *fine motor skills*, such as drawing, handwriting and assembling small objects;
- *self-help skills*, such as dressing, toileting and travelling independently;
- *communication skills*, such as clarity of speech, vocabulary and length of sentences;
- *basic academic skills*, such as reading, writing, spelling and number skills;
- *work habits*, such as concentration span and study skills;
- *play/leisure skills*, such as hobbies and sporting activities;
- *behaviour outside school*, such as in the home, on family outings;
- *relationships*, such as with parents, siblings, other family members, friends.

Reviews

Pro-formas for parents to complete beforehand can also be used to improve parents' participation in reviews of their children's progress. An example of this is provided by Hughes and Carpenter (1991) who describe the development and use of a Parents' Comments Form (PCF) intended to help parents organize their thoughts on their child's progress and needs so that they could contribute more meaningfully to the annual reviews of the child's Statement of special educational needs. In an evaluation of the use of the PCF, with parents of children attending a special school for children with severe learning difficulties, it was reported that parents found the forms helpful in preparing for the review meetings and it was considered that this led to a more effective partnership between parents and teachers. Clearly, pro-formas which parents can use to provide information on their children as part of a review of their progress will need to be designed to take children's ages and any special needs into account. However, most pro-formas will seek comments from parents about changes in the following areas since the previous review:

- *child's health*: for example any significant illnesses, changes in medication or diet;
- *behaviour*: any significant problems either in the home or outside it;
- *abilities*: any significant difficulties or progress made;
- *likes and dislikes*: current likes and dislikes which the child expresses;
- *independence*: any significant progress towards independence;

- *priority areas*: any weaknesses which need to be overcome or strengths to develop;
- *home circumstances*: anything which may be affecting the child's behaviour at school.

SUMMARY AND CONCLUSIONS

Reviews of the literature and personal experience have provided convincing evidence of the effectiveness of parental involvement in promoting children's learning and modifying their behaviour. The origins of parent involvement have been traced to early intervention programmes such as Project High/Scope and the Portage Project whose use continues to increase in popularity throughout the world. Another area of children's education in which parents have long been involved is reading. Three approaches to parent involvement in reading were described: parent listening; paired reading; and Pause, Prompt and Praise. Behavioural training of parents is another aspect of parent involvement which has a fairly long history. Its focus on reducing behaviour problems and remediating children's learning difficulties was described. More recent, in this country, has been the involvement of parents in assessments of children and reviews of their progress. What parents want out of assessments and can contribute to them was discussed and strategies for improving parental input into the assessment and review processes were described.

Chapter 5

Interpersonal Skills for Working with Parents

Several years ago I led a five-day workshop with parents of schizophrenic young people in Lisbon, Portugal. On the first day I arranged the parents in a circle and asked them to share their personal stories with each other, myself and my co-leader, who also acted as translator. The second parent to speak was a mother who quickly became tearful and said that her situation was so hopeless that the only way out she could see was to kill her son and then kill herself! The group listened to her story for around 30 minutes, after which a father volunteered that he had had similar thoughts years ago but had somehow managed to carry on. He didn't offer any advice but did give her something to think about, which was translated to me as, 'It is raining today. Tomorrow the sun may shine.'

I wasn't too sure that there would be such a change in the weather for this mother who appeared to be in deep despair for the remainder of the first day. I wondered whether she would turn up for the second day. To my relief, she did turn up and, in fact, started the second day by announcing that she felt a lot better. She had worked out a plan of action for dealing with the problems which her son presented and came across as a much happier and more confident person. When I asked what had brought about this change she said that it was hearing all the other parents' stories and being able to express her most frightening feelings which had helped her to see things more positively. This story, therefore, reinforces the importance of expressing feelings and of being listened to as well as the value of sharing experiences with other people in a similar situation to oneself.

Many teachers will have heard stories of, or experienced themselves, situations in which people have found out by chance just how helpful it is to have someone *listen and understand* when the other person has a concern they need to talk over. Teachers cannot fail to be aware of the importance of listening in education, since listening skills are enshrined in one of the attainment targets in the English National Curriculum. How is it, then, that when parents are asked how they would like teachers to change, the most common response is that they would like them to listen more? Somehow, our knowledge of the importance of listening doesn't get translated into practice.

In order to work effectively with parents, teachers need to have good inter-personal communication skills. While teachers typically have excellent skills in the areas of verbal presentation, explanation and information-giving, they generally have less well-developed skills in the areas of listening, counselling and assertiveness (Seligman, 1979; Turnbull and Turnbull, 1986). These three skill areas are particularly important for working with parents and therefore are the focus of this chapter.

Probably the most important of the three sets of skills are the ones needed for effective listening. These include the skills of attentiveness, passive listen-ing, paraphrasing and active listening. Other interpersonal skills, which are needed for communicating with parents and for collaborating with colleagues, are assertion skills. These include techniques for making and refusing requests, giving constructive feedback, handling criticism, and problem-solving.

Also essential are basic counselling skills, particularly if set within a problem-solving model of counselling which involves listening and assertion skills. To use such a model teachers must first of all *listen* to what parents have to say, in order to help them clarify their concerns or ideas. Parents should then be helped to gain a clear *understanding* of the problem situation which they face or goal which they have. Finally, teachers should help parents decide what, if anything, they want to do about their concern or idea: that is, what *action* they wish to take. Possessing the skills required to implement this simple model of counselling will contribute enormously to the ability of teachers to establish a productive working relationship with parents. A three-stage problem-solving counselling model is presented later in this chapter, fol-lowing the discussion of listening and assertion skills.

LISTENING SKILLS

A discussion of the skills required for effective listening to take place is pre-sented below. The major components of listening are: attentiveness; passive listening; paraphrasing; and active listening (Bolton, 1979; Brammer, 1993).

Attentiveness

Effective listening requires a high level of attentiveness. This involves focusing one's physical attention on the person being listened to and includes several components.

Eye contact
The importance for the listener of maintaining good eye contact cannot be over-emphasized. While parents are talking they may not look directly at the teacher for most of the time but will occasionally look across to check that he or she is listening. Therefore, it is important to maintain eye contact through-

out the interview. In situations where someone feels uncomfortable with direct eye contact it is usually satisfactory for the listener to look at the speaker's mouth or the tip of their nose instead. Speakers generally cannot tell the difference.

Facing squarely
To communicate attentiveness it is important for the listener to face the other person squarely or at a slight angle. Turning one's body away from another person suggests that you are not totally with them.

Leaning forward
Leaning slightly forward towards the person being listened to communicates attentiveness. Alternatively, leaning backwards gives the impression that you are not listening.

Open posture
Having one's legs crossed, or even worse, one's arms crossed when one is listening gives the impression of a lack of openness, as if a barrier is being placed between the listener and the person talking. Attentiveness is best communicated by the adoption of an open posture with both arms and legs uncrossed. However, many women feel most comfortable sitting with their legs crossed at the knees and would not be able to remain as relaxed with their legs uncrossed. This does not significantly reduce their attentiveness.

Remaining relaxed
It is essential to be relaxed while adopting an attentive posture, since if the posture adopted is not comfortable, it is not possible to concentrate fully on what is being said. Therefore, it is important to take up an attentive posture in which one feels relaxed, even if this doesn't exactly follow the guidelines discussed above.

Appropriate body motion
It is important to avoid distracting movements such as looking at the clock, fiddling with a pen, or constantly changing position. In addition, it is important to move appropriately in response to the speaker, since a listener who sits perfectly still can be quite unnerving and may not communicate attentiveness.

Non-distracting environment
It is not easy to listen attentively in an environment in which there are distractions. The room used should be as quiet as possible and the door should be kept closed. Telephone calls should be put on hold and a 'Meeting in Progress' sign hung on the door. Within the room the chairs used should be comfortable and there should be no physical barrier such as a desk between teacher and parent.

Distance

There needs to be a suitable distance between speaker and listener. If the distance is too great or too small then the speaker will feel uncomfortable and this will impede the communication. A distance of about three feet is usually recommended, but this can vary between cultures, so it is best to always look for signs of discomfort or anxiety in the listener and adjust the distance accordingly.

Passive listening

Passive listening involves using a high level of attentiveness combined with other skills. These are: invitations to talk; non-verbal grunts; open questions; attentive silence; avoiding communication blocks; and minimizing self-listening.

Invitations to talk

Before the teacher can begin to listen, parents need to be invited to talk about their concern or idea. For example, 'How can I help you?' or 'You seem upset. Would you like to talk about it?' The specific wording of the invitation needs to be tailored to the situation and people involved.

Non-verbal grunts

There are various sounds or short words which are often known as 'non-verbal grunts', because they let the speaker know that you are with them without interrupting the flow. For example, 'Go on', 'Right', 'Huh Huh', 'Mm Mm'. It is particularly important to use these while listening to someone on the telephone because the speaker cannot gauge the listener's attentiveness through the usual visual clues.

Open questions

Open questions are used for clarification or to encourage the speaker to continue. For example, 'How do you mean?' or 'What happened then?' Closed questions, which usually require a very brief response such as 'Yes' or 'No' and allow the listener to set the agenda, are avoided. This can be very hard for teachers to do since they typically spend much of their time in classrooms asking closed questions and it is difficult to change this strategy quickly.

Attentive silence

Teachers should pause for a few seconds after each thing they say to give parents the opportunity to say more or to remain silent. During silences, parents are often clarifying their thoughts and feelings. Therefore, using attentive silence is a very effective way of encouraging people to open up and continue exploring their concerns or ideas.

Avoiding communication blocks

Certain types of comment tend to act as blocks to the communication process and therefore must be avoided (Gordon, 1970). When used they stop parents from exploring their concerns and ideas. Common examples are: *criticism*, *sarcasm*, *advice giving*, or *reassurance*, such as saying, 'Don't worry, it will work out all right.'

Another type of block which is particularly annoying to parents is denial or false acknowledgement of feelings, such as suggesting that parents should 'Look on the bright side' or telling them 'I know exactly how you feel.'

Other common blocks involve diverting parents from the topic, either directly or by the use of excessive questioning or by excessive self-disclosure when people go on about themselves or others they have known who have had similar problems. Further blocks involve moralizing, ordering or threatening; that is, telling parents what they ought or must do. Finally, there are the blocks in which diagnosis or labelling are used. For example, telling someone that they are 'a worrier'. All the blocks tend to stifle the exploration of concerns or ideas and therefore should be avoided.

Minimizing self-listening

Self-listening occurs when people drift off into their own thoughts rather than listening to what the other person is saying. When a teacher is listening to a parent and begins to self-listen there is a likelihood that important aspects of what is said will be missed. The teacher may then become confused and will be unable to respond effectively to the parent, who will therefore become aware of the inadequacy of the listening and tend to clam up. This is why it is very important that, when teachers are listening to parents, they are able to reduce self-listening to a minimum. The best way of minimizing self-listening is to use the listening techniques discussed below.

Paraphrasing

Paraphrasing is a skill which most people already use to some extent. When someone has told us something important and we want to be sure that we have understood correctly, we feed back the main points of the message to the person for his or her confirmation. This is a crude form of paraphrasing which is similar to that used by competent listeners.

An effective paraphrase has four components. First, the paraphrase feeds back only the key points of the speaker's message. Second, paraphrasing is concerned with the factual content of the speaker's message, not with feelings. Third, an effective paraphrase is short and to the point. It is a summary of the speaker's key message, not a summary of everything said. Fourth, a paraphrase is stated in the listener's own words but in language which is familiar to the speaker.

Paraphrases are used when there are natural breaks in the interaction, such as when the speaker pauses and looks at the listener or when the speaker inflects his or her voice at the end of a sentence, clearly wanting some response from the listener. At this point the listener feeds back the essence of the speaker's message and then waits for a response. When the paraphrase hits the mark the speaker typically indicates that this is the case by saying 'That's it' or 'Right' or 'Yes' or by some non-verbal means such as nodding his or her head.

If the paraphrase is not accurate, or only partly accurate, then the response will not be so positive and in most cases the speaker will correct the listener. In so doing the speaker will also be clarifying for himself or herself exactly what is meant, so the paraphrase will still have been of value.

Active listening

Active listening generally involves trying to understand what the person is feeling and what the key message is in what they are saying, then putting this understanding into your own words and feeding it back to the person (Gordon, 1970). Thus, active listening involves the listener being actively engaged in clarifying the thoughts and feelings of the person they are with. It builds on attentiveness, passive listening and also paraphrasing, in that the main aspects of what is being communicated are reflected back to the person. This is done to provide a kind of 'sounding board' to facilitate exploration and clarification of the person's concerns, ideas and feelings.

Gordon (1970) suggested that certain attitudes are essential prerequisites to active listening. These are:

- the listener must really want to hear what the other person has to say;
- the listener must sincerely want to help the other person with his or her concern;
- the listener must be able to respect the other person's feelings or values even though they conflict with his or her own;
- the listener must have faith in the other person's ability to work through and solve his or her own problems;
- the listener must realize that feelings are transitory and not be afraid when people express strong feelings such as anger or sadness;
- the listener must accept that other people may have very different opinions, attitudes and values to themselves.

The process of active listening involves reflecting both thoughts and feelings back to the speaker. The speaker's key feeling is fed back along with the apparent reason for the feeling. When teachers are learning how to use active listening it is useful to have a set formula to follow. The formula 'You feel ... because ...' is typically used.

For example: 'You *feel* frustrated *because* you haven't finished the job'; 'You *feel* delighted *because* she has done so well.'

When teachers gain confidence in their use of active listening the formula is no longer needed and thoughts and feelings can be reflected back in a more natural way.

For example: 'You *are* angry *about* the way you were treated'; '*You're* sad *that* it has come to an end'; 'You *were* pleased *with* the result'; 'You *were* annoyed *by* her manner.'

However, active listening involves much more than simply using this formula. It requires the listener to set aside his or her own perspective in order to understand what the other person is experiencing. It therefore involves being aware of how things are said, the expressions and gestures used and, most importantly, of hearing what is not said but which lies behind what is said. The real art in active listening is in feeding this awareness back to the person accurately and sensitively. This, of course, is very difficult, but the beauty of active listening is that you don't have to be completely right to be helpful. An active listening response which is a little off the mark typically gets the person who is talking to clarify his or her thoughts and feelings further. However, active listening responses which are way off the mark suggest to the speaker that the other person isn't listening and therefore can act as blocks to communication.

ASSERTION SKILLS

Assertiveness involves being able to stand up for one's own rights while respecting the rights of others; being able to communicate one's ideas, concerns and needs directly, persistently and diplomatically; being able to express both positive and negative feelings with openness and honesty; and being able to choose how to react to situations from a range of options.

Teachers need assertion skills both for working with parents and for collaborating with their colleagues. Teachers will have to deal with criticism or aggression from time to time and will need to make and refuse requests. They will also need to be able to give constructive feedback. Finally, they will need to be able to help people solve problems. The skills involved in these situations are outlined below and are discussed in more detail elsewhere (Hornby, 1994b; Bolton, 1979).

Basic elements of assertiveness

There are three aspects of assertiveness which apply in any situation. These are: physical assertiveness; vocal assertiveness; and assertion muscle levels.

Physical assertiveness
Assertive body language is a key component of effective assertion. The components of physical assertiveness are similar to those of the attentiveness required for effective listening: an open posture, facing the other person squarely, standing or sitting erect or leaning slightly forward, maintaining good eye contact, not fidgeting or using superfluous gestures. What is different about assertiveness is that the facial expression should match the seriousness of the message and also that feet should be firmly planted on the floor, even when sitting.

Vocal assertiveness
To optimize the effectiveness of the message the voice should be firm but calm. It is best to speak a little more slowly than usual but at a normal volume

and to breathe deeply as this will help to ensure that there is enough breath to speak firmly and to maintain calmness.

Assertion muscle levels
Whenever one is being assertive it is important to select the appropriate strength or 'muscle level' of the assertive response used. Usually, one should start at the lowest muscle level, or assertion strength, which is likely to achieve success. For example, 'I would appreciate it if you could …' If this doesn't work the muscle level is increased and the request repeated. For example, 'It is important that you …' Muscle levels are then progressively increased until a satisfactory response is obtained. For example, from 'It is essential that you …' to finally, 'I demand that you …'

At the same time that verbal muscle levels are being increased, physical and vocal assertiveness should also be gradually made more intense: that is, by using a more serious facial expression and a firmer tone of voice with each increase in muscle level.

Responding to criticism

Teachers will occasionally get criticism from their colleagues and sometimes from parents. Important factors involved in determining the impact of criticism are the intention of the person giving it and whether it comes with constructive suggestions for change. Holland and Ward (1990) have described a four-step approach which is useful in considering how to respond to criticism. The four steps of the model are outlined below.

Step one: Listening to the criticism
Listening skills are useful in clarifying the criticism. Open questions such as, 'How do you mean?' or 'Can you be more specific?' are helpful in finding out exactly what the criticism is aimed at.

Step two: Deciding on the truth
Before responding to the criticism, its validity should be considered. It may be completely true, partly true or completely untrue. One's assessment of the validity of the criticism will determine the response used in step three.

Step three: Responding assertively
If we consider the criticism to be completely true then it is best to agree with the criticizer, make a brief apology and assure them you will correct the situation. For example, 'I'm sorry about not consulting you on this matter. I'll make sure it doesn't happen again.'

If we consider the criticism is partly true then we should agree with the part considered to be valid, briefly apologize, and at the same time correct the part which is false. For example, 'Yes, I did make a mistake in that case and I regret that, but I don't accept that I'm making mistakes all the time these days. I make occasional errors like anyone else.'

If we consider the criticism to be completely false then we should clearly reject it, tell the other person exactly how the criticism makes us feel, ask for an explanation of their comments and make an affirmative statement about ourselves. For example, 'I don't agree that I was wrong in that case and am greatly offended by the suggestion. What grounds could you possibly have for making such a comment? My relationships with pupils are excellent.'

Step four: Letting go
Decide to use what you have learned from the criticism and about the criticizer and move on. I know this is much easier said than done, but we mustn't let ourselves be deflected from our goals by what is, after all, just one person's opinion.

Dealing with aggression

Occasionally teachers have to deal with aggressive behaviour from parents or colleagues. Kroth (1985) has provided some guidelines for what teachers should do and should not do in this situation.

Teachers should not:

- argue with a person who is behaving aggressively;
- raise their voices or begin to shout;
- become defensive and feel they have to defend their position;
- attempt to minimize the concern which the other person is expressing;
- take responsibility for problems which are not of their making;
- make promises which they won't be able to fulfil.

All of these responses are ones which are commonly used by people confronted with aggression, but they seldom work and are more likely to make the other person more aggressive. The following responses are far more likely to calm the other person down and lead to a constructive resolution of the situation.

Teachers should:

- actively listen to the other person, reflecting back their thoughts and feelings in order to confirm that they are listening and to help them understand the other person's perspective;
- speak softly, slowly and calmly;
- ask for clarification of any complaints which are vague;
- ask them what else is bothering them in order to exhaust their list of complaints;
- make a list of their concerns. Show them the list and ask if it's correct and complete;
- use the techniques of problem-solving, discussed below, to work through their list of concerns in order to resolve the problems or conflicts, starting with the one of highest priority to the other person.

Refusing a request

Teachers will sometimes receive requests from parents or colleagues which they think they shouldn't agree to but feel unable to turn down. People have difficulty saying 'No' for several reasons, but especially due to the fear that it will damage their relationship with the other person. The alternative to agreeing to requests you would rather turn down is to use acceptable ways of saying 'No', several of which are listed below.

The explained 'No'
When you have a genuine reason for the refusal you can say 'No', explain why you are turning down the request, and give a brief apology. For example, 'No, I'm sorry, I can't make it because I'm already booked for that day.'

The postponed 'No'
In this refusal you explain that you can't comply with the request at present but may be able to in the future. For example, 'No, I'm sorry, I'm not able to take that on today, but I may be able to help you with it in the future.'

The delayed 'No'
In this technique you ask for time to think it over. This gives you the opportunity to consider carefully whether you want to comply with the request and to work out exactly how you will say 'No'. For example, 'I'm busy right now and I'd like to give it some thought. Can I get back to you tomorrow?'

The listening 'No'
In this refusal active listening skills are used to let other people know that you understand the reason for their request. The listening response is combined with a brief apology and a firm refusal. For example, 'Yes I understand your frustration about not being able to get the job done. I'm sorry, but I can't help you with it.'

The 'Get back to me' 'No'
This involves explaining the difficulties you have in complying with the request, then suggesting that the person try elsewhere and if all else fails to come back to you and you'll see what you can do. 'For example, 'I'm busy for the next two weeks so I suggest you try elsewhere. If you really get stuck I'll do my best to fit you in but I can't promise anything.'

The 'broken record' 'No'
This is a form of refusal which is particularly useful for dealing with people who won't take 'No' for an answer. It involves making a brief statement of refusal to the other person, avoiding getting into discussion with them, and simply repeating the statement as many times as necessary (like a broken record) until the message gets across.

Making a request

Teachers sometimes need to request various things from their colleagues and occasionally need to make requests of parents. So, being able to make requests effectively is important, especially since many people find it difficult to do. Manthei (1981) has provided some useful guidelines for making requests and these are outlined below.

- *State your request directly* – state your request firmly and clearly to the other person.
- *Say exactly what you want* – be specific and precise about your requirements.
- *Focus on the positive* – create an expectation of compliance.
- *Answer only questions seeking clarification* – don't allow yourself to be side-tracked.
- *Allow the person time to think about it* – suggest you'll get back to them tomorrow.
- *Repeat the request* – use the 'broken record' technique to restate the request.
- *Be prepared to compromise* – you are better off getting partial agreement than rejection.
- *Realize the other person has the right to refuse* – respect the other person's rights.

Giving constructive feedback

Giving constructive feedback to others is an important skill for both our professional and personal lives. Whereas criticism is mostly given without the intention of helping the other person, constructive feedback is aimed at helping them to function better. A model for providing constructive feedback which I have found extremely useful is one that I adapted from the DESC script popularized by Bower and Bower (1976). DESC stands for: describe; express; specify; and consequences. This is a technique which professionals find valuable in giving feedback to parents of children with special needs and also to their colleagues and which, in addition, parents find extremely useful in handling difficulties with professionals. The four steps involved in using the modified DESC script are described below.

1. *Describe.* Describe the behaviour of concern in the most specific and objective terms possible. For example, 'When you change teaching programmes without consulting me ...'
2. *Express or explain.* Either express your feelings about this behaviour or explain the difficulties it causes for you, or do both, calmly and positively, without blaming or judging the other person, or 'putting them down'. For example, 'I get very annoyed (express) because parents may become confused and even lose confidence in us (explain).'
3. *Specify.* Specify the exact change in behaviour required of the other

person. For example, '. . . So, in future, will you make sure you consult me before making such changes . . .'

4. *Consequences.* The consequences which are likely to result from the other person complying with the request are stated. The benefits for both people are stated first, along with any concessions which you are willing to make. For example, '. . . then we will be able to maintain our excellent working relationship and parents will be clear about our teaching programmes'.

If the other person is not willing to comply, then the modified DESC script should be repeated at progressively higher muscle levels, with the highest muscle level including the negative consequences for the person of not complying with the request. For example, '. . . If you do not consult me as I suggest then I will have to insist on all your teaching plans being formally submitted to me for approval.'

Preparation and delivery
Although the modified DESC script is simple enough to be thought up and delivered on the spot, it is usually best to write it out beforehand. It is then possible to make sure that the wording is the most appropriate and also to rehearse it with a third person in order to get feedback on it. It can then be decided when, where and how it will be delivered.

Problem-solving

Often teachers find that their opinions differ from those of parents or their colleagues. This can lead to a deterioration in relationships unless these difficulties are resolved. Bolton (1979) has proposed a model for collaboration in solving problems which is useful in this situation. The six steps of the model are described below.

1. *Define problem in terms of needs of each person.* This involves the use of active listening in order to clarify the other person's needs and, if possible, to understand the reason for these needs. It also involves stating one's own needs assertively. This is a key element of the model and may take up half of the total time required for the process.
2. *Brainstorming possible solutions.* Once both persons' needs are understood brainstorming can be used to seek solutions which meet both sets of needs. First, as many potential solutions as possible should be listed, without attempting to evaluate or clarify any of them. Wild ideas should be included, as these often spark off more creative solutions. Then, each other's ideas should be expanded on and clarified.
3. *Select solutions which meet both parties' needs.* A choice is then made from the list of potential solutions, the one which best meets the needs of both parties. This will probably involve discussing the relative merits of several solutions in meeting each other's needs.
4. *Plan who will do what, where and by when.* It may be useful to make a

written note of the decision about what each party will do, where it will be done and when it will be completed by.

5. *Implement the plan.* It is clearly important that each party should attempt to follow the agreement closely in implementing the plan.
6. *Evaluate the process and the solution.* An essential part of the problem-solving process is to agree a time when both parties can meet to evaluate how well the solution is meeting each of their needs.

COUNSELLING SKILLS

The counselling model which is proposed for use with parents is based on a general approach to counselling which can be used with children and adults in a wide variety of situations. The model involves a three-stage approach to counselling with stages of *listening, understanding*, and *action planning*. It is a problem-solving approach to counselling adapted from previous models by Egan (1982) and Allan and Nairne (1984) and is presented in more detail elsewhere (Hornby, 1994b).

As was suggested earlier in this chapter, *some* parents will be in need of supportive counselling. However, the majority of these parents will not ask for counselling directly, but will typically go to teachers with concerns about their children. If teachers use listening skills in order to help parents explore their concerns then the parents' need for help will emerge. This is when teachers should be able to help parents by providing the counselling that they need. Parents are much more likely to be willing to talk about their concerns with someone who is working directly with their child, such as a therapist or teacher, than with a professional counsellor whom they do not know. What teachers need therefore is a counselling model which is practical, simple to learn and easy to use. A summary of the model proposed is presented in Figure 5.1.

Stage	Listening	Understanding	Action planning
SKILLS	Attentiveness	Structuring	Brainstorming options
		Summarizing	Evaluating options
	Passive listening	Identifying themes	Action-planning skills
		Expressing implications	
	Paraphrasing	Information-giving	Assertion skills
		Suggesting alternative interpretations	
		Suggesting new perspectives	Reviewing skills
	Active listening	Goal-setting	Termination skills

Direction of movement in counselling process
⟶

Figure 5.1: Counselling model

The rationale for using such a model is based on the idea that any problem or concern which parents bring to counselling can be dealt with by taking them through the three stages of the model in order to help them find the solution that best suits their needs. First of all, the teacher uses the skills of the *listening* stage to establish a working relationship with parents, to help them open up and to explore any concerns they have. Then the teacher moves on to the second stage, using the skills of the *understanding* stage in order to help parents get a clearer picture of their concerns, develop new perspectives on their situation, and suggest possible goals for change. Finally, the teacher moves on to the third stage, of *action planning*, in which possible options for solving parents' problems are examined and plans for action are developed. Thus, different skills are needed at each stage of the model: skills for listening in the first stage, skills for understanding in the second stage, and skills for action planning in the third stage. These are discussed below.

Skills for listening

The first stage of the model involves the use of the listening skills which were described earlier in this chapter. *Attentiveness* and *passive listening* are used to establish a rapport in order to help parents open up. *Paraphrasing* and *active listening* are used to help parents explore their concerns and ideas.

Skills for understanding

The second stage of the model involves the use of skills designed to increase the parents' understanding of their problem situation. Skills used to help parents get a clearer picture of their concerns include:

- *structuring*, which involves keeping parents focused on key aspects of their concern;
- *summarizing*, which involves feeding back to parents an overview of their key thoughts and feelings;
- *identifying themes*, which involves feeding back to parents any common themes, connections or contradictions running through their account of the problem situation;
- *expressing implications*, which involves drawing tentative conclusions about the parents' situation and linking this with the possible implications of these conclusions;
- *information-giving*, which involves teachers sharing with parents, either from their experience of children with special needs or from other knowledge relevant to the parents' situation.

Skills used to help parents develop new perspectives on their situation include: *suggesting alternative interpretations*, which involves suggesting objective explanations for past events to counter the negative interpretations which parents are sometimes held back by; and *suggesting new perspectives*, which involves helping parents to consider more constructive ways of viewing their situation.

Finally, in order to help parents develop possible goals for change, the skill of *goal-setting* is used. This involves helping parents decide on the major aspect of their situation which needs to be focused on and considering potential changes which are desirable and feasible.

Skills for action planning

The third stage of the model involves the use of action-planning skills in order to help parents consider possible options for solving their problems, develop plans for action and review the progress of these plans. The skills used to help parents consider possible options for change are the same ones used in the problem-solving model discussed earlier in this chapter. They include the skills of *brainstorming options* and *evaluating options*.

Once parents have decided on their preferred option, *action-planning* skills are used to help them develop concrete plans for implementing this option. In addition, parents may be taught some of the *assertion skills* discussed earlier in this chapter, in order to help them implement this plan.

Next, *reviewing skills* are used in order to help parents to review the progress of these plans. This involves arranging for further contact in order to evaluate parents' progress with their plans. If there has been insufficient progress then the process can be recycled and parents once more taken through the three stages of the model in order to develop a new action plan.

Finally, *termination skills* are used to refer parents on for more specialist help, or to bring to a close a successful series of contacts, while communicating to parents that they are welcome to return to discuss other concerns or ideas at any stage in the future.

SUMMARY AND CONCLUSIONS

Teachers need to have good interpersonal communication skills in order to work effectively with parents. Listening, assertion and counselling skills have therefore been elaborated in this chapter. The skills required for effective listening which were discussed include attentiveness, passive listening, paraphrasing and active listening. The assertion skills which were described include techniques for making and refusing requests, giving constructive feedback, handling criticism and problem-solving. The basic counselling skills which were discussed were set within a three-stage problem-solving model of counselling which involves listening, understanding, and action-planning skills.

Previous research which I have carried out suggests that teachers are generally more competent at the skills involved in stages two and three of this model, which focus on understanding and action planning, than they are at the skills involved in stage one, which involves listening (Hornby, 1990; Hornby and Peshawaria, 1991). However, the same research showed that these teachers were able to significantly improve their listening skills and thereby become competent in using the three-stage model with parents in a 30-hour in-service training course. Therefore, it is not unreasonable to expect all teachers to be provided with the opportunity of developing competence in these interpersonal skills. Possession of high levels of the skills discussed in this chapter will enable teachers to work effectively with parents using the wide range of strategies which are discussed in this book.

Chapter 6

Parent Education

The importance of parent education first became clear to me when I was teaching adolescents with moderate learning difficulties in a secondary school special class in New Zealand 25 years ago. This is illustrated by two incidents involving my pupils' parents, one which I had some success with and the other which left me feeling very frustrated.

First, there was Grant, who was 15 years old but had a reading age of around 6 years and couldn't tell the time or handle money at all. On the first class outing into Auckland, for which the pupils caught buses from their homes into the centre of the city, Grant didn't turn up. When I visited him at home that evening his parents told me that he wasn't allowed to catch a bus by himself as they didn't think he could manage it. I then spent considerable time convincing Grant's parents that he needed to learn how to catch buses by himself and that he could learn to do so. After much discussion about Grant's difficulties and his future they agreed to let him catch the bus, under my supervision, the next time we had a class trip into Auckland.

After several rehearsals in class of what he needed to do, on the day of the next class trip Grant set out from home to catch the bus, with me watching him every step of the way. I watched him leave his house and walk to the bus-stop, wait for the correct bus to come and then get on it and give the driver his fare. I then drove into the city centre to await the bus's arrival. When the bus pulled in and Grant climbed off, the look of accomplishment on his face suggested he'd done much more than simply catch his first bus: he beamed as if he'd just gone round the world by himself!

This was a big step for Grant but an even bigger one for his parents because it made them realize that he was ready to tackle quite grown-up things by himself. From then on I was able to continue to provide guidance to his parents in order to help Grant become as independent as possible. In fact, when he left school it was to start a job on the other side of the city to his home, for which he had to change buses in the centre of Auckland. But this was by then well within Grant's capacity.

The second incident involved Stephen who was also 15 but was more able than Grant and had a reading age of around 9 years. This incident occurred when Stephen's parents didn't turn up to a parent–teacher meeting. As I was concerned about Stephen's somewhat bizarre behaviour at school, I telephoned to suggest that, since I would pass their house on my way home from the meeting, if it was convenient, I could visit so that we could discuss his progress. This was agreed and I subsequently found myself deep in discussion with Stephen's parents about his childhood, his interests, his current behaviour and especially about what the aims of his educational programme should be. I found out that Stephen's father was very keen for him to learn maths and spent time each evening drilling him in such things as fractions and decimals. I tried tactfully to suggest that some of this work was too difficult for Stephen and that there were other, more important things he could be learning. However, when I left the house, at one o'clock in the morning, his father's last words to me were, 'There's a flagon of whiskey in that cabinet and when Stephen passes his School Certificate in maths it'll be opened.'

Needless to say, I found this very depressing. Stephen was as likely to pass this academic maths exam as he was to walk on water! But his father's comment had confirmed that I had not convinced him that there were a lot more useful things for Stephen to be learning. In fact I never did get through to his father, and Stephen's behaviour continued to be somewhat bizarre. The fact that I could make no impact on this situation made me feel very frustrated: my attempts at educating this parent about the needs of his son had failed.

These and other similar incidents, which occurred while I was teaching the special class, convinced me of the importance of parent education. It was my successes in working with some of the parents which made me realize the potentially huge benefits to children of teachers working closely with their parents. But it was my inadequacy in situations like the one with Stephen's father which made me realize that working effectively with parents was not easy and needed much more knowledge and skill than I had at that time.

These practical experiences gave me the incentive to learn more about working with parents. When I asked senior people in the education field in New Zealand about how I could address the block I had encountered with Stephen's father, one suggestion I was given was that getting parents together in groups might be helpful. But at that stage the concept of group parent education was totally foreign to me. In fact, I became involved in group work with parents quite by chance. When, a few years later, I was working as a trainee educational psychologist, I noticed that there were six referrals from parents whose children attended the same large primary school. They all wanted guidance on managing their children's behaviour, so I decided to see them in a group. I did this mainly to save time, but as the sessions progressed it became clear that parents were finding it very useful to be able to discuss their problems within the group and, as a result, I became more and more convinced of the value of the group approach to parent education.

Then a friend, who was a teacher at a special school for children with severe learning difficulties, suggested that the parents there would also benefit from group work which focused on managing their children's behaviour. I then began to team up with colleagues in order to run groups for parents of children with severe learning difficulties at several special schools in Auckland (Hornby, 1980). This led naturally to providing group programmes for parents of children with other difficulties such as hearing impairment, physical disability (Hornby and Murray, 1983), heart defects and mental illness.

The benefits of these parent workshops have convinced me of the value of group parent education programmes in providing support and guidance to parents. The aim of this chapter is, therefore, to describe various types of parent education programmes and discuss key aspects such as group leadership skills and group dynamics, so that teachers can learn how to provide such experiences for parents.

BENEFITS OF GROUP WORK WITH PARENTS

Probably the most important benefit of working with groups of parents is that, in talking with others, parents realize that they are not the only ones with problems. This sharing of common problems typically leads to parents feeling that they are all 'in the same boat', which is a particularly therapeutic component of group work (Yalom, 1985). In addition, parents can express their feelings regarding their children and discover that others have similar feelings, which often helps them come to terms with their own. Further, in a group with other parents it is often easier for them to reveal concerns which they have not felt able to bring up individually.

Another benefit of group work is that parents experience mutual support from the other group members which helps them to become more confident in their own ability as parents. The group also provides the opportunity to practise communication skills such as the expression of feelings and the ability to listen empathically to others (Dinkmeyer and Muro, 1979). A further benefit of group work is that when parents participate in a group they learn together in a mutually supportive atmosphere. They are often more responsive to changing their opinions and learning new strategies in this situation (Kroth, 1985). Also, in a group, parents are exposed to a wider range of behaviour problems and learning difficulties, and the techniques used to deal with them, which may facilitate their handling of similar problems encountered in the future.

Another benefit is that, in a group, solutions for a particular parent's difficulties will be suggested by other parents who may have experienced similar difficulties in the past. Parents are almost always responsive to such potential solutions. Groups also provide numerous possibilities for modelling and role play of difficult situations and are a source of ideas for potential reinforcers, motivation, and social reinforcement (Rose, 1977).

There are also advantages for the teachers of working with groups of parents. Obviously, since more parents can be reached in a group than individually, it is possible to help a greater number of parents than could be managed using an individual approach. Also, there are times when several parents are experiencing the same difficulty and teachers can provide guidance to them all at the same time rather than individually, thereby using their time more efficiently. Another advantage is that, because of the efficient use of time in group work, it is possible to justify two or more professionals working together with the group of parents and thereby sharing skills and knowledge with each other. In addition, the parents in the group are a source of knowledge and skills which professionals can utilize. Working with parent groups is a powerful way to educate teachers about parents' experiences and needs.

However, there are some negative aspects of doing group work with parents. Some parents do not feel comfortable being in a group with other parents and prefer to receive guidance individually. Also, in order to obtain maximum participation in group work with parents it is often necessary to hold sessions in evenings or at the weekend, which can cut into teachers' leisure and preparation time. Finally, working with groups of parents requires skills and knowledge over and above what is needed for individual work, so these need to be acquired to a reasonable level before embarking on group work with parents (Seligman, 1990). Group leadership skills and knowledge of group dynamics are discussed next.

GROUP LEADERSHIP SKILLS AND KNOWLEDGE

The skills needed to lead parent education groups include those which were discussed in Chapter 5; that is, counselling skills, assertion skills and, most importantly, listening skills. The skills required in order to lead such groups are more comprehensive than those needed for individual work with parents. Dinkmeyer and Muro (1979) agree that, first and foremost, group leaders need to be skilled listeners. They suggest that leaders also need to be able to develop trust within the group and to maintain a focus on the goals of both the group as a whole and of the individuals within it; further, that leaders need to be spontaneous and to be responsive to what is happening within the group at any point in time. They need to be able to combine the ability to stand firm with a good sense of humour. Finally, to be effective, they need to be perceived by group members as being *with them* as a group and *for them* as individuals.

Another perspective on leadership skills which I have found particularly useful is that provided by Trotzer (1977) who considers that group leaders need the skills of *reaction*, *interaction* and *action*. These are briefly outlined below.

The *reaction skills* which leaders need are:

- *listening*: in order to communicate respect, acceptance, empathy and caring;
- *restating*: to convey to group members that they are being heard;
- *reflecting*: in order to convey understanding and help members to express themselves;
- *clarifying*: in order to better understand confusing aspects of what is said;

- *summarizing*: to provide an overview, stimulate reactions and move on to new ground.

The *interaction skills* which leaders need are:

- *moderating*: to ensure that all group members have the opportunity to talk;
- *interpreting*: to help members gain insight into what is happening within the group;
- *linking*: to tie together common elements within the group and promote cohesiveness;
- *blocking*: to prevent undesirable action by one or more group members;
- *supporting*: to encourage members to share of themselves safely within the group;
- *limiting*: to prevent actions which would infringe the rights of group members;
- *protecting*: to prevent group members from being unduly criticized or hurt;
- *consensus taking*: to help members see where they stand in relation to others.

The *action skills* which leaders need are:

- *questioning*: to help members consider aspects they had not thought of;
- *probing*: to help members look more deeply into their concerns;
- *tone setting*: to establish an atmosphere and qualitative standard to be adhered to;
- *confronting*: to help members face things about themselves which they are avoiding;
- *personal sharing*: to show that the leader is human and is prepared to open up;
- *modelling*: to teach members interpersonal skills such as active listening.

Group dynamics

In addition to these skills, group leaders also need to have a good understanding of group dynamics; that is, the processes which occur within groups. There are several models of the process of group development and each suggests that all groups need to pass through several stages or phases if they are to function well and achieve their goals. The various models differ in the number of stages included and in some of the characteristics of the stages, but there is considerable overlap (for example see Corey, 1990 and Trotzer, 1977). The one which I have found most useful in understanding what happens in groups is that proposed by Williamson (1982), which has four stages: *inclusion*; *work*; *action*; and *termination*. These are outlined below.

Inclusion
The first stage of any group is one of developing a group cohesiveness so that all members feel a part of the group. Participants need to feel comfortable

about belonging to the group. They need to be willing to share aspects of them-selves and to explore concerns and issues within the group. Some time will be needed for this to develop as members tentatively interact with the leader and each other. As this process develops, group norms or implicit group rules will begin to be established.

Work
The second stage is one in which the members begin to work on resolving the concerns or issues related to the purpose of the group. This is usually the longest stage in the group's life. It involves members in discussing ideas, expressing feelings and listening to others in order to gain insight into their own situation. It is in this stage that group members will experience the greatest benefit. However, some members will resist change and there will be conflict and tension within the group. At the same time relationships between other group members will deepen and become more meaningful. The work stage can be regarded as providing a transition between members becoming part of the group and deciding what action to take.

Action
In the third stage, the understanding and growth which occurs in the work stage needs to be translated into some form of action, otherwise the group will not fulfil its purpose. Individual members, or the group as a whole, need to decide what action to take to address the concerns which brought them into the group. Since change is difficult for members to cope with, the group needs to provide them with considerable support during this stage.

Termination
The final stage is one in which the group comes to a close, with members expe-riencing a sense of completion, accomplishment and gratitude for what the group has helped them achieve.

When groups progress through these four stages then the experience can be a very powerful one in promoting learning and personal growth in the members. I have observed this happen on numerous occasions with parents who have participated in parent workshops. The growth in confidence of many parents over the period of these projects has often been startling. Unfortunately, however, because groups can be so powerful, when they are badly led they can result in members having their self-confidence threatened. So it is essential to ensure that qualified and experienced leaders are employed for any group work carried out with parents.

PARENT EDUCATION GROUPS

Since the 1970s interest in attending courses in parent education from parents in general has grown steadily in the USA, but has been much slower to develop in other countries. Several programmes for group parent education using quite different approaches have been developed and disseminated. The approaches described in this section are Parent Effectiveness Training, Parent Behavioural Training and some other less widely used programmes.

Parent Effectiveness Training

Parent Effectiveness Training is the most widely disseminated parent education programme in the Western world, with hundreds of thousands of parents having participated in it. It is based on the book of the same name which became an international bestseller for the author, Thomas Gordon (1970). The aim of the programme is to facilitate communication and improve relationships between parents and their children. The programme consists of an eight-week course attended by ten to twelve parents with a leader who has been trained in leading PET groups. The methods used by leaders are a combination of demonstration and role play of the skills being taught, with open discussions conducted in a circle.

The programme focuses on four key aspects of parent–child relationships. First, parents are taught listening skills so that they can improve their ability to listen to their children. The most essential aspect of this is learning active listening, the skill which was discussed in Chapter 5. Second, parents are taught how to express their feelings using 'I' messages in order to avoid using 'You' messages which tend to put the blame on their children. Third, parents are taught how to analyse ownership of a problem so that they can decide which are their problems and which should be left with the child. The importance of allowing children to accept ownership of problems which belong to them is emphasized. Fourth, for problems whose ownership lies with both parents and children, parents are taught how to use a six-step method for resolving the conflict, which is called 'no-lose problem solving'.

There are numerous positive reports of the effectiveness of PET in improving parents' relationships with their children, but the results of reviews of the more rigorous studies are less convincing (Rinn and Markle, 1977).

Other forms of parent education

There are several other forms of group parent education programmes. Two of the better known of these will now be briefly described in order to demonstrate the wide range of approaches which are available. Systematic Training for Effective Parenting (STEP) is a programme based on the ideas of Alfred Adler (1927) which have been developed into a parent education kit by Dinkmeyer and McKay (1976). The aim of STEP is to help parents develop a better understanding of their children's behaviour, improve communication with them and increase parents' influence over their children's behaviour. The STEP kit includes a leader's manual; charts which illustrate the main concepts to be taught; group discussion guideline cards; and cassette tapes with brief lectures and skill-building exercises for parents. Key aspects of the programme are study of the *goals* of children's behaviour and the application of *natural consequences* to deal with misbehaviour.

The Transactional Analysis approach to parent education is based on the ideas of Berne (1964) and Harris (1969) which have been applied to children by Babcock and Keepers (1976). The aims of group parent education based on this approach are to increase parents' understanding of their relationships with their children and thereby to improve communication within the family. Key concepts in this approach are the 'ego states' of *parent, adult* and *child* which are highlighted in family communication and the complementary, crossed and ulterior transactions which occur within families. Also important are the 'basic life positions' adopted by individuals and the unconscious 'games' played by family members. Sessions include both didactic and experiential components. Relevant reading and practical homework assignments are used, and specific problems brought to the group by participants are discussed and brainstormed within the group.

No research evaluations of either STEP or the TA approach to parent education could be found in the literature, so it must be assumed that although these are promising approaches, their effectiveness in improving parent–child relationships has not been demonstrated.

Behavioural Group Training

Behavioural Group Training (BGT) is an extension of the principles of Parent Behavioural Training (discussed in Chapter 4) to work with groups of parents. It is a widely used approach to parent education with parents of children with behavioural problems and other kinds of special needs. The aim of BGT is to teach parents the principles and practice of behavioural analysis in order to improve their management of their children's behavioural and learning difficulties. BGT typically consists of an eight- to ten-week course attended by six to twelve parents and led by psychologists trained in behavioural methods. The training techniques used by the leaders include: lectures; modelling; role play; parent training manuals; discussion; and homework assignments.

BGT programmes typically include the concept of positive reinforcement of appropriate behaviour, as well as discussion of the different types of reinforcers which parents can use and conditions for their effective use. Also covered are other techniques used to increase levels of appropriate behaviour such as stimulus control, contingency contracting and Premack's Principle. In addition, techniques used to decrease levels of inappropriate behaviour are taught, such as differential reinforcement, extinction, time out, response cost and over-correction. Finally, programmes aimed at parents of children with special needs also tend to include techniques used to develop new skills such as task analysis, shaping and backward chaining.

Research conducted to evaluate the effectiveness of BGT has presented some evidence to support the suggestion that parents do learn behavioural principles and techniques and are able to apply these with their children (Graziano and Diament, 1992; Hornby and Singh, 1983, 1984).

Combining different approaches

In a review of the field of parent education Tavormina (1974) found that most approaches could be classified as either reflective or behavioural. In reflective parent education programmes, such as Parent Effectiveness Training, the focus is on the parents' emotional needs. Parents are encouraged to discuss their concerns and opinions and express their feelings about their children. The aim is to help parents to understand and come to terms with the parenting role and thereby improve their ability to relate to their children. In behaviourally based parent education programmes, such as Group Behavioural Training, the focus is on teaching parents skills. Parents are taught behaviour modification techniques in order to facilitate the management of their children's behaviour and thereby improve parent–child relationships.

In a landmark study which compared the effectiveness of these two approaches with parents of children with special needs, Tavormina (1975) reported positive outcomes for both reflective and behavioural groups. In a further study it was found that a combination of reflective and behavioural approaches was the most effective (Tavormina *et al.*, 1976).

Group work with parents of children with special needs has generally taken the form of either reflective counselling (Hornby and Singh, 1982) or behavioural training (Hornby and Singh, 1983). However, positive outcomes have been widely reported when aspects of the reflective and behavioural approaches have been combined in workshops for parents of children with special needs (Attwood, 1978, 1979; Cunningham and Jeffree, 1975; Hornby, 1992).

A parent workshop model which combines aspects of both reflective and behavioural approaches was developed in New Zealand in the 1980s (Hornby, 1987). The aim of this project was to develop the format for a parent workshop which combines group guidance in the form of brief lectures with group counselling conducted by means of small-group discussions. It was considered that this format would provide a supportive environment in which parents could learn new skills and gain confidence through talking with other parents. The workshop has been used with groups of parents of children with a wide variety of types of special needs, including the physically disabled, visually impaired, hearing impaired, intellectually disabled and those with heart defects. The workshop format is one which can be adapted for use with parents with a wide range of concerns such as:

- parents of bereaved children;
- parents of sick children;
- single parents;
- parents with step-families;
- parents of children with emotional or behavioural difficulties;
- parents of teenagers;
- parents of pre-school children.

Details of the parent workshop are presented below so that teachers can adapt it to suit the population of parents with whom they work.

ORGANIZATION OF PARENT EDUCATION WORKSHOPS

A summary of the main aspects of workshop organization is presented below.

Recruitment

The best method of recruiting parents for workshops is by sending a letter of invitation to all parents likely to be concerned with the topic being addressed whose children are attending the school. No form of selection has been found necessary in the past, as parents for whom workshops are not suitable have tended not to participate from their own choice.

Venue

A venue which is familiar to the parents, comfortable and easy for parents to get to is best. School staff-rooms are a popular choice of venue for smaller workshops.

Sessions

Between six and eight, weekly, two-hour, evening sessions have been found to be the most satisfactory. Fewer than six sessions is insufficient for parents to benefit from the therapeutic process which the group will experience as the workshop progresses. More than eight sessions is often too great a commitment of time and too tiring for parents and teachers alike. Anything greater than a one-week break between sessions, such as fortnightly or monthly sessions, leads to a considerable drop in attendance and therefore should be avoided. Evening sessions are generally easier for both professionals and parents to attend, but weekends can also be used. Two hours is considered to be the optimum time for the length of sessions. Any less leaves insufficient time for both discussion and lecture presentation.

Number of parents

A reasonably large number of parents can be catered for by taking the group of parents as a whole during the introduction, lecture presentations, and final summary sections of the workshop and dividing them into small groups during the discussion section. The size of the small groups needs to be large enough to give a reasonable range of children and problems, but small enough to provide sufficient time for each parent to discuss his or her concern. About six to ten parents is generally the most satisfactory size.

Group leaders

Small-group discussions need to be led by professionals with previous experience of leading such groups. Teachers with no experience can be involved as co-leaders who work in tandem with the leader. In this way teachers can be trained to lead their own groups in subsequent parent workshops.

Format of workshops

Workshops are typically divided into four parts: introduction; lecture presentation; small-group discussion; and summary. These are outlined next.

Introduction
The first fifteen minutes of workshops are used to help parents relax, since many of them experience anxiety when they first come along to group sessions where they are expected to talk about their children. It provides an opportunity for parents to get to know other parents and teachers informally and also overcomes the problem of late arrivals interrupting the lecture presentation.

Lecture presentation
Lectures of a maximum of twenty minutes in length are presented to the whole group of parents who are usually seated in a horse-shoe arrangement around the speaker. The topics of the lectures are best determined by sending out a list of potential topics beforehand and asking parents to choose. Where necessary, relevant specialists can then be invited in to give some of the lectures. Clearly the lecture topics will depend on the needs of the children whose parents are involved in the workshops. For example, lecture topics used in workshops for parents of children with disabilities have included: speech and language development; behaviour management; social and emotional development; sexual development; services available; recreational activities; and vocational placement.

Small-group discussion
The largest block of time in the workshop, of over an hour, is given over to discussion which is conducted in small groups. Discussions are conducted in separate rooms, with chairs arranged in a circle. Groups usually consist of a leader, a co-leader and six to ten parents. Leaders guide the discussions using the skills discussed earlier in this chapter.

Co-leaders work in tandem with leaders by focusing on the group dynamics and on the body language of group members so that they can draw the leader's attention to a parent who may want to say something but hasn't been noticed. Leaders and co-leaders should meet for half an hour before each session to plan the session, and for a short time afterwards in order to debrief and discuss the subsequent sessions.

Summary
With all the parents present a leader or co-leader from each small group reports back on the issues and concerns discussed in their group. Any handouts, such as a summary of the lecture content for that session, are distributed and homework tasks, such as the completion of behaviour observation forms, are explained.

It is important to conclude the formal aspects of each session punctually since many parents will have arranged baby-sitters and need to be home promptly. However, it has been found that some parents will remain to talk with other parents or professionals for up to half an hour afterwards.

OTHER TYPES OF GROUPS

Various other types of programmes have evolved in order to cater for the needs of parents and other family members. Self-help groups and advocacy groups have emerged to support parents of children with a wide range of difficulties. In addition, workshops have been developed to address the needs of other members of families who have children with various special needs; that is, siblings, fathers and grandparents. Also, parent-to-parent schemes aimed at providing support and guidance to parents of children with special needs of various kinds have been developed in several countries. All involve an educative focus facilitated by some form of group work and are outlined below.

Self-help groups

A major growth area in mental health services in recent years has been the proliferation of self-help groups, well-known examples of which are Alcoholics Anonymous and Weight Watchers (Gitterman and Shulman, 1986). Groups for parents have been no exception and in most cities around the world there are now self-help groups for parents of children with most types of special needs. These range from groups in which a small number of parents get together regularly for support, to others which have become national organizations such as MENCAP and CRUSE.

Many of the therapeutic factors associated with group work, referred to earlier in this chapter, also work to promote personal growth in self-help groups. In such groups parents develop their own personal coping strategies and increase their social support networks.

Advocacy groups

A type of group training for parents which has emerged recently is programmes for training parents in advocacy skills (Schilling, 1988). The aim of advocacy training is to help parents to become advocates for their own children in order to obtain the best possible services for them and ultimately to become advocates for people with special needs in general. Advocacy training involves gaining information about the rights of parents and their children and about how to access the resources and services available to them. It also involves parents learning the assertion skills which were discussed in Chapter 5, so that they can overcome any lack of confidence and advocate for their children assertively rather than aggressively.

Advocacy training programmes therefore typically consist of a combination of professional input and parental sharing about available resources and how to access them, plus the teaching of assertion skills through didactic presentations, along with modelling and role play of the relevant strategies. In these ways professionals are able to pass on to parents the knowledge and skills they need, thereby empowering parents to become as effective as possible in their task of parenting their children.

Parent-to-parent schemes

Another type of parent group which has shown rapid growth in numbers in recent years are parent-to-parent schemes. Parent-to-parent schemes are support services for parents of children with special needs in which support is provided by a team of volunteer parents who themselves have children with special needs (Hornby, 1988; Hornby *et al.*, 1987). Up to this time most schemes have been organized for parents of children with disabilities, but the parent-to-parent model is applicable to parents of children with a wide range of special needs.

Typically, parent-to-parent services operate as a telephone contact helpline. Schemes are advertised by means of leaflets, posters or cards put on notice boards in places where parents are likely to see them, such as libraries, health centres and schools. Parents seeking contact ring the helpline telephone number and are put in touch with a support parent who has a child with similar difficulties.

Potential support parents are initially recruited by means of contact with existing parent groups and other organizations such as MENCAP or CRUSE. The parent-to-parent training course is typically conducted in a series of eight weekly sessions of two hours each. A maximum of twelve parents can attend each course. The training course focuses on the sharing of parents' own experiences and the learning of active listening and other helping skills, as well as on the organization of a parent-to-parent service including such issues as the distribution of publicity materials and the planning of a duty roster for telephone duties.

Grandparent workshops

Workshops for grandparents of children with special needs are generally of one day's duration and include either a guest speaker invited to address matters of concern to grandparents or a panel of parents or siblings to talk about their experiences. Time is also scheduled for grandparents to meet in small groups, facilitated by a professional, to share their concerns and feelings. The workshops can therefore provide opportunities for grandparents to meet each other, as well as to obtain information from professionals about their grandchildren's special needs, and guidance on how to best provide support for the family (Vadasy *et al.*, 1986).

A related development is the Helping Grandparent Programme in which experienced grandparents are trained in order to provide support to grandparents of newly diagnosed children (Sonnek, 1986). This scheme is based on the parent-to-parent model which was described above.

Fathers' programmes

Fathers' programmes generally use a workshop format, meeting, for example, every two weeks on Saturday mornings (Meyer *et al.*, 1985). There are typically three components to fathers' programmes, the first two of which are similar to those in workshops for parents and grandparents. First, guest speakers provide fathers with information about their children's special needs and the services available. Second, discussion groups are used to enable fathers to discuss their concerns and interests with other fathers and thereby obtain peer support. Third, fathers bring their children along to the meetings so that part of the time allocated can be used for all the fathers and children to get together and take part in group activities or individual play. The aims of this component of fathers' programmes are both to encourage fathers to interact more with their children and to provide their wives with some respite from child-care responsibilities (Vadasy *et al.*, 1985).

Sibling workshops

Sibling workshops are aimed at providing siblings of children with special needs an opportunity to meet others in the same situation, to gain specific information on special needs, and to learn how to handle common incidents which occur in families which have a member with a special need of some kind (Meyer *et al.*, 1985b). Sibling workshops have followed a similar format to the workshops described above but have also included outings and activities aimed at providing enjoyment for siblings themselves. In order to help the younger children open up about their worries and feelings, some different activities can be included. For example, siblings are asked to write down their problems on paper which is put in a box and is later taken out and read out to everyone and discussed in the group, without identifying the writer.

SUMMARY AND CONCLUSIONS

In this chapter it has been proposed that there are substantial benefits for parents of participating in parent education programmes and various other types of group work. The group leadership skills and knowledge of group dynamics needed in order to lead group work with parents were discussed. Various forms of parent education were described, including Parent Effectiveness Training and Group Behavioural Training. A parent workshop model which is considered to be useful for parents of children with a wide range of difficulties and needs was described in detail. Brief descriptions of other forms of groups such as parent-to-parent schemes, sibling workshops, fathers' programmes and self-help groups were provided.

Chapter 7

Helping Parents of Children with Disabilities and Illnesses

During my first few months of working as an educational psychologist in New Zealand I was asked to see a 4-year-old girl who was causing concern at the kindergarten she attended. The problem was that Meeka became hysterical whenever her mother attempted to leave the kindergarten. The teachers had done all they could to distract Meeka and involve her in activities with the other children, but she would just sit and cry until her mother returned. After observing Meeka while the teachers once more tried unsuccessfully to keep her attention while her mother slipped away, I wondered if the problem was something more than simple separation anxiety. I therefore decided to see Meeka again, but this time at my office so that I could observe her further, talk to her mother and do a developmental assessment.

Results of the assessment, observations of Meeka's behaviour and a developmental checklist completed by questioning her mother all suggested that Meeka was functioning intellectually at around a 2-year level. Thus, her development was found to be significantly delayed and she fell within the range for which children could be considered for placement in special pre-school facilities for children categorized in New Zealand as 'intellectually disabled'. I discussed this possibility with Meeka's mother who agreed to visit some of the special facilities for which she was eligible. I arranged for us to visit three special pre-schools which were within reasonable travelling distance of the family home.

On the appointed day I collected Meeka, her mother and her maternal grandmother from their home and we set off to check out the three schools. We talked to staff and observed children in the first two schools while Meeka clung on to her mother, who clearly had some reservations about each of them. At the third school, as the adults talked, Meeka left her mother to play on the equipment with the other children. After a few minutes it was clear that she was having a wonderful time and fitted in perfectly. Mother and grandmother were convinced, after talking to the headteacher and seeing Meeka fit in so well, that this was the place for her. The headteacher said that a place was available so she could start on the following Monday. Meeka actually cried when her mother went to take her back to the car – she wanted to stay and play.

I dropped everyone back home and went back to the office to do the necessary paperwork. I think I was still slapping myself on the back for a job well done at Monday lunchtime when the headteacher of the special pre-school phoned our office. She told us that Meeka's father had just been to visit and had withdrawn her because he 'didn't want his daughter going to a school for handicapped kids'.

I had made two very important mistakes. First, I had seen Meeka's mother several times and even met her grandmother but I had never talked with her father, either about the results of the assessment or about her placement in a special pre-school. I had overlooked the fact that most children have two parents who are both concerned about their education and care. Second, I had also not realized that by passing on the assessment results and by suggesting the special pre-school placement I was effectively diagnosing a severe learning difficulty in a child whose parents had apparently not considered the possibility that their child had any sort of disability.

What I should have done, as soon as possible after I did the assessment, was to arrange a meeting with both parents to discuss the results. This should have been done in private, with Meeka present. I should have explained the possible implications of the results as sensitively and objectively as I could and given her parents the opportunity to absorb all this and ask any questions they wanted to. I should have been prepared to provide the parents with up-to-date information about their daughter's special needs and the various services and voluntary agencies which could be of help to them. I should have been ready to help the parents consider the various options for Meeka's educational placement. Finally, I should have been sensitive to the fact that her parents may not have been able to take all this in during one meeting and would need further meetings in order to come to terms with the situation and plan effectively for Meeka.

But I did none of these things because I never arranged to see Meeka's father. The consequences of this were that her parents were left to struggle with the implications of the diagnosis of their daughter's disability which caused considerable distress for them and other members of the family. Fortunately, Meeka's mother had involved her mother in attempting to sort out her grand-daughter's difficulties and in visiting the special pre-schools. I understand that it was she who persuaded her son-in-law to allow Meeka to return to the school a few days later.

This case taught me the importance for teachers and other professionals in the field of education of considering the effects of a child's special needs on the whole family. When a child has a serious illness or disability it affects not only the parents but also other members of the family, such as siblings and grandparents, as well as friends. This chapter considers the effects on families, and their members, of children with disabilities and medical conditions, and provides guidelines for teachers in their work with parents whose families are experiencing either of these situations.

In this chapter, a model of adaptation to children's special needs will be described, along with other perspectives on the process which parents typically experience in coming to terms with the discovery that their child has a serious illness or a disability. The various perspectives on the process of parental adaptation are provided in order to alert teachers to the wide range of reactions which parents may experience. Of course, how parents react to and cope with the discovery that their child has special needs will differ from parent to parent. The various models and perspectives are presented in order to describe possible parental reactions, not to suggest that all parents will necessarily experience some or any of them. Later in the chapter, consideration will be given to how children with disabilities or illnesses typically affect and are affected by the functioning of these families and the broader social context. Teachers need to understand these issues in order to be able to provide effective help to these parents and to optimize their involvement in the education of their children.

COMING TO TERMS WITH A CHILD'S SPECIAL NEEDS

Most teachers have had significant losses or traumatic events in their lives, such as the death of someone close to them, and appreciate that these have involved them experiencing emotional reactions which were often surprising and sometimes quite frightening. They will also remember that these experiences sometimes led to them questioning their philosophical beliefs and values. Following major trauma or losses they will have been faced with new tasks or challenges. They will realize that we gradually learn to live with these major events in our lives, though they are not forgotten and feelings are retriggered at various times in the future. They will also be aware that the way we react to such trauma is different for each individual.

Discovering that your child has special needs resulting from a serious illness or a disability is a traumatic event for most parents. In a way it represents a loss of the normal, healthy child they thought they had, coupled with uncertainty about many of their expectations for the future. For example, will their children be able to live a normal life, get a job, get married, or even be able to care for themselves well enough to be able to live away from the family home? The discovery that their child has special needs therefore generally leads to parents experiencing similar feelings and thoughts to those which are typical following any major trauma or loss. Four different models have been proposed to explain the process which parents experience in coming to terms with a child who has special needs. Each of these models explains a different aspect of the process and is therefore important in gaining a thorough understanding of what parents experience. The models to be described are ones which focus on:

- stages of emotional reaction;
- the re-experiencing of grief;
- an examination of philosophical beliefs and values;
- a series of tasks or challenges.

These are discussed below.

Stages of emotional reaction

I have developed a model for the process of coming to terms with a child's special needs which I have found useful both for helping parents to talk about their reactions and feelings, and for increasing teachers' awareness of the process which parents may be going through. The model is similar to stage models of adaptation to disability described by several writers (Bicknell, 1988; Gargiulo, 1985; Hornby, 1982; Seligman, 1979). In this model (presented in Figure 7.1) it is suggested that the process of adaptation to the diagnosis of a disability or medical condition can be viewed as a continuum of reactions, beginning at the time of the initial diagnosis, through which people pass in order to come to terms with it.

Figure 7.1: Model for coming to terms with loss

The visual representation of the model for adaptation illustrates the continuum of stages of reaction beginning with shock and passing through denial, anger, sadness, detachment and reorganization until the person achieves a mature emotional adjustment to the situation.

The initial reaction of most parents on being informed of their child's disability or medical condition is typically one of *shock*. Parents report feeling confusion, numbness, disorganization and helplessness and are typically unable to take in much of what they are told at this time. The shock reaction usually lasts from a few hours to a few days. When this reaction has subsided, parents are more able to take in information and are generally keen to learn as much as they can about their child's condition and what can be done to help.

Shock is typically followed by a phase characterized by *denial* or disbelief of the reality of the situation. At first, many parents find it difficult to believe that their child has a problem. They may think that there must have been a mistake. It is understandable that they would want a second opinion, and this option should be made available to them. However, for a few parents this leads to them 'shopping around' in an attempt to get a more favourable diagnosis, which, if found, will probably retard the adaptation process. This is why it is important that teachers are honest with parents and don't try to give them a prognosis which is too hopeful or unrealistic. Neither, of course, should they paint too bleak a picture. Feedback from many parents has convinced me that the main qualities which they need from professionals at this time are sensitivity and honesty. They want us to tell them exactly what we know and what we don't know. It is also very confusing for parents when professionals disagree about the diagnosis or prognosis and this can therefore reinforce their denial and retard the adaptation process.

As a temporary coping strategy denial can be quite useful in giving parents time to adjust to the situation. It is only when denial is prolonged and intense that it is problematic. Some denial is probably present throughout the adaptation process, and even when parents have apparently come to terms with their child's special needs there may still be an element of denial present. Teachers should therefore be sensitive to the degree to which parents will use denial to cope with their reactions to the situation. Teachers can help parents to overcome their use of denial by listening to them and sensitively providing them with objective information about their children's development and progress. Confronting the denial is seldom a useful strategy as it usually results in parents becoming anxious and rejecting the teacher rather than accepting the reality of the child's needs.

Following denial, when they are beginning to accept the reality of the situation, many parents experience *anger* about the loss. They may search for the cause of the problem or for someone to blame. If it is a chronic illness, then there may be an investigation of the family histories of both parents to find out whether there have been other members of the extended family who have had the same condition. If there is, then a parent's anger may be displaced onto their spouse. Alternatively, underlying the anger may be feelings of guilt about somehow being responsible for their child's problem. For example, if it is a disability which has been caused by an accident, parents may wonder what they could have done to prevent it occurring. Parents who experience anger as part of the adaptation process need to express it in order to move forward. Teachers need not therefore take such anger personally or label parents as aggressive, but they do need to be willing to encourage parents to express and explore their angry feelings and to be able to use active listening in order to help them in this task.

Sadness typically follows anger and is a reaction which, more than any other, pervades the whole adaptation process. This sadness can be due to parents grieving for the loss of the healthy child which they thought they had, or it can be due to sadness about the loss of opportunities and ambitions which their children may not be able to fulfil. Either way, sadness, depression and in some cases even despair, are understandable reactions of parents to finding out that their child has a serious problem. Some parents have told me that they spent a lot of time crying. Others have reported that they felt so bad they couldn't face meeting anyone and tended to cut themselves off from social contact for a long time. For many parents sadness and depression are a normal part of the adaptation process. They must therefore not be labelled as clinically depressed on the basis of experiencing this reaction for a reasonable period of time.

Following sadness, parents typically experience a sort of *detachment*, when they feel empty and nothing seems to matter. Life goes on from day to day but it has lost its meaning. The appearance of this reaction is considered to indicate that the parent has begun to reluctantly accept the reality of the loss. It is therefore thought to be a turning point in the adaptation process.

Reorganization is the reaction which follows detachment. It is characterized by realism about the situation and hope for the future. Parents begin to focus more on what their children may achieve and less on what they may miss out on. When parents have reached this stage they are typically more interested in participating in parent education programmes and joining support groups, so it is a good time to give parents the opportunity of attending parent programmes of various kinds. Being actively involved in facilitating their children's development and meeting up with other parents who have children with similar problems often helps parents to feel better about the whole situation and therefore is useful in helping parents make progress towards adaptation.

Finally, parents are considered to reach a point when they have come to terms with the situation and exhibit a mature emotional *acceptance* of the disability or medical condition. They are fully aware of the child's special needs and strive to provide for these. However, children are treated, as much as possible, as just another member of the family, which does not revolve around them.

Of course, in reality, the adaptation process is not as clear-cut as simply moving from stage to stage would suggest. One reaction may be uppermost at a particular time, but certain amounts of the other reactions involved in the process will also be present. For example, when a person's main reaction is one of anger they will also be experiencing a fair amount of denial and sadness at the same time, and lesser amounts of the other reactions will also be present. Also, sadness and grief are considered to be the over-riding feelings experienced and are ones which, more than any other, pervade all stages of the adaptation process.

Many parents say that they have experienced feelings associated with more than one stage at certain times. Some apparently did not experience a particular stage, while others report being fixated at one stage for a considerable time before being able to move on. Some people say that they experienced the stages in a different order. A few parents report that they are not aware of experiencing different reactions at different times. Thus, the process appears to be qualitatively different for each person.

Some parents may partially work through the adaptation process in anticipation of the loss. Confirmation of their child's problem by a professional is accompanied by feelings of relief for these parents. This appears to happen most often with parents of children with hearing impairment or specific learning difficulties, such as dyslexia, who have had difficulty getting professionals to make a definite diagnosis.

The adaptation process is considered to be a normal healthy reaction to the discovery of the child's disability or illness and can be viewed as a form of grieving similar to that which follows any traumatic loss (Worden, 1991). Some parents appear to work through the process in a few days, whereas others seem to take years to reach a reasonable level of adaptation. It is generally considered that most people will take around two years to come to terms with the diagnosis of a disability or serious illness. However, some parents seem to take longer and a few possibly never fully adjust to the situation.

Passage through the adaptation process can be accelerated or retarded by what parents do and by what professionals, such as teachers, say to them. Parents who refuse to accept their child's disability and do not allow themselves to experience the feelings triggered by their loss will take much longer to come to terms with the situation. To use the terminology of grief therapy, parents need to do the 'grief work' associated with their loss in order to adjust to it (Worden, 1991).

Professionals can also slow down parents' progress through the adaptation process by being insensitive and thereby reinforcing parents' anger which can then become a fixation, since being angry is one way of avoiding facing up to the sadness associated with any loss. Passage through the adaptation process can also be retarded by professionals who suggest unrealistic prognoses which often result in parents becoming stuck in the denial stage, clinging on to unrealistic hopes of what their child might achieve.

Re-experiencing the grief

The fact that feelings associated with parents' reactions to the disability or illness can be re-triggered at various times in the future has led some writers to suggest that, rather than a grieving process which can be worked through with feelings to some extent resolved, parents of children with special needs experience 'chronic sorrow' (Olshansky, 1962; Wikler *et al.*, 1981). It is suggested that the reactions which are evoked, such as anger, sadness and denial, are not fully resolved but become an integral part of the parents' emotional life (Max, 1985). Thus, there will be various occasions when these reactions may be re-experienced. This reworking of parental reactions can occur at various transition points in the child's development, such as school entry, the onset of puberty, leaving school and leaving home (Wikler, 1981 and 1986). It can also occur when parents are told about an additional problem at some time later than the original diagnosis. For example, Featherstone (1981) recounts how, having apparently come to terms with her child being blind, she was devastated when mental handicap was later diagnosed.

Examination of philosophical beliefs and values

Experiencing any serious trauma or major loss can lead to a person questioning their religious or ideological beliefs and re-thinking the values which they hold most dear. Roos (1978), who is a parent of a child with a disability as well as being professionally involved in the disability field, suggests that many parents of children with special needs experience various fundamental existential conflicts. The existential conflicts identified by Roos include *disillusionment*. He considers that experience gradually erodes the high expectations which people develop as children, leading to disillusionment with ourselves, others, and life in general. Many people therefore channel their unrealistic expectations into their children. However, a child with a disability or serious illness is often an unsuitable vehicle for fulfilling these expectations and therefore can provoke a feeling of disillusionment.

Another conflict Roos calls *aloneness*. The fact that one is ultimately alone in one's passage through life is something that everyone must eventually come to terms with. Many people, however, attempt to avoid dealing with this conflict by establishing intimacy with their children. Since this may be more difficult to do with some children, for example those with learning difficulties or communication problems, parents are often forced to face up to their existential loneliness. *Vulnerability* occurs because, as people mature, they lose childhood fantasies of the omnipotence of their parents and themselves and begin to realize the tenuousness of their control over life, and therefore their personal vulnerability. Diagnosis of disability or serious illness in a member of the family can be a painful reminder of this vulnerability.

A conflict about *inequality* occurs because children grow up with the notion that fairness and justice ultimately prevail in life. Therefore, when faced with a child with special needs in the family, people may feel overwhelmed with the enormity of the apparent inequity, which can present a challenge to their ethical and religious beliefs. Also, maturity brings with it the realization of personal *insignificance*. Most people strive to find some meaning in life, typically through fulfilling satisfying social roles such as husband and father. When they are frustrated in achieving a rewarding parental role, perhaps because the child has a communication problem, parents may find it difficult to achieve meaning in their lives and therefore become vulnerable to feelings of insignificance.

Another conflict Roos terms *past orientation*. Thus, while most parents anticipate their children's future with enthusiasm, parents of children with disabilities or serious illnesses tend to view the future with apprehension. Hence, whereas most people are future-oriented, such parents typically focus on the present or the past. Finally, he suggests that *loss of immortality* is another conflict. He explains that a common approach to coping with anxiety about one's own death is to seek symbolic immortality through one's children. When a child is disabled or has a serious illness, however, this potential avenue to immortality is threatened. Particularly when the child is an only child, parents may be forced to face up to this existential conflict.

Series of tasks and challenges

Another way in which the adaptation process can be viewed is to consider that it presents a number of challenges over and above those faced by parents whose children do not have special needs (Mitchell, 1985). Parents of children with disabilities or medical conditions are seen as needing to address a series of tasks, each of which must be at least partially mastered if they are to come to terms with the situation. The major challenges and tasks for such parents are listed below.

- *First*, parents must accept the reality of their child's disability or medical condition and come to terms with their own reactions to the situation and to the reactions of family, friends and the wider community.

- *Second,* parents must gain an understanding of the nature of their child's special needs and learn skills for facilitating the child's development.
- *Third*, parents need to learn how to access relevant health, education and welfare services and establish working relationships with the professionals involved with their child.
- *Fourth*, parents need to learn how to participate appropriately in decision-making regarding their child's educational placement, medical treatment, future training and work placement.
- *Fifth*, parents need to identify individuals and groups who can provide them with support and to build up a support network.
- *Sixth*, parents must establish a positive parenting relationship and learn to cope with the day-to-day tasks of caring for their child with special needs.
- *Seventh*, parents must be able to maintain their self-esteem despite the difficulties they encounter and maintain a positive relationship with their spouse in order to establish a balanced family and personal life.
- *Eighth*, parents must be able to accept their children's right to independence, such as the expression of their sexuality and their need to live outside the family home.
- *Ninth*, parents must organize provision for their children with special needs for the future when parents may become ill or die.
- *Tenth*, parents must be able to help the child understand his or her disability or medical condition and adapt to living with this in the community.

Knowledge of the specific tasks which parents of children with special needs have to address enables teachers to be aware of the kinds of issues which these parents may be dealing with, in addition to those of other parents, at various stages of the children's development. Further understanding which teachers need to develop in order to work effectively with parents involves knowledge of the ways in which families function, which is discussed in the following section.

EFFECTS ON AND OF FAMILY

Family systems perspective

Families are considered not only to be affected by children with special needs but also to have a significant impact on them (Bell, 1968; Mink and Nihira, 1987). Therefore, the type and severity of the child's illness or disability are likely to play an important role in how parents are affected. For example, a child with a serious illness will generally have a different impact on the family to a child with a disability. Likewise, a child with cancer will have a different impact to one with asthma, and a child with a severe learning difficulty will affect the family differently to a child with dyslexia. In addition, the kind of people parents are will have an important bearing on the child's behaviour and development. Parents' personalities, coping strategies and the state of their health will also affect the child.

As children with special needs pass through different developmental stages, they will also affect their families in different ways. For example, an infant with a disability or behaviour problem will have a different impact on parents than an adolescent with a similar condition. Likewise, the effect parents have on their child with special needs will depend on the particular stage in the life cycle which they are in. For example, a child who is the first-born child of young, recently married parents is in a very different position to a child with the same kind of special need who is born to older parents who already have several other children. The younger of these families is likely to experience higher levels of stress and have more difficulties in coping than the larger, more established family.

When teachers have children with special needs in their classes it is important for them not to lose sight of the fact that each child is a member of a family which will be affected by, and affect, the child. In fact, it is now believed that the behaviour of individual family members is strongly influenced by the functioning of the family system of which they are a part (Berger and Foster, 1986). Therefore, a change in the family system will inevitably lead to a change in the behaviour of each of the family members. For example, when one parent leaves the family home or dies, all other family members will be affected, and teachers can therefore expect to see changes in the behaviour of the children they have in their classes.

Likewise, a change in an individual's behaviour will cause the family dynamics to change. The implication of this is that what happens to a child with special needs at school will have an impact on the whole family to which that child belongs. Therefore, the whole family system needs to be taken into account when considering the effects of an intervention on an individual family member, since the treatment of individual children, without taking their families into account, may result in an increase in problems experienced by the family as a whole (Chilman *et al.*, 1988). For example, the transfer of a child with special needs from a special school to a mainstream school placement will have an impact not only on the child but also on other members of the family. A knowledge of family systems theory therefore provides an excellent rationale for teachers to always consider the child's family and, wherever possible, to work closely with parents in planning educational programmes.

Ecological model

It is now considered that children's development and behaviour cannot be understood independently of the social context in which they occur. The social environment influences the behaviour of children and families, and this occurs at several levels. Thus, the effects on parents of caring for a child with any kind of special need are strongly influenced by the social environment in which they are living, including the extended family, the education system, the services available and community attitudes. This is illustrated by the Ecological model of family functioning, adapted from that described by Bronfenbrenner (1979), which is presented in Figure 7.2. The model includes four

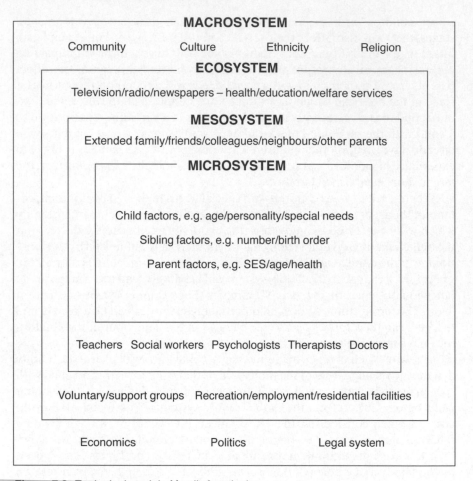

Figure 7.2: Ecological model of family functioning

different levels of influence on the family: the microsystem; the mesosystem; the exosystem; and the macrosystem.

Microsystem
The family of a child with a serious illness or disability is considered to constitute a microsystem, with the child, parents and siblings reciprocally influencing each other. How well this nuclear family functions therefore depends on variables associated with each of its members. First, features of the special need itself such as the type, severity and when it was diagnosed will have an influence. For example, a medical condition, such as a heart defect, which can be diagnosed shortly after birth can have a very different impact on the family to a learning difficulty which is usually not diagnosed until much later. It is generally considered that a special need which is diagnosed early in the child's life is easier to come to terms with than one that is diagnosed later, since

parents will have believed for several months or even years that the child was normal in every way and may find it difficult to change this belief. The severity of the special need is also an important factor. A child with a severe learning difficulty is likely to have a different impact on the family to one who has a specific learning difficulty such as dyslexia. Also, uncertainties about the diagnosis which often occur with disabilities such as dyslexia, autism and mild to moderate levels of learning difficulty can be more difficult for families to come to terms with than in clear-cut cases such as Down's syndrome.

Second, factors associated with the child with special needs and his or her siblings will have an influence on family functioning. Whether the child is the first born, last born, a middle child, an only child or a twin will have an impact on the family. The ages and personalities of children and their siblings will also play a big part in how well the family functions. A young baby with a disability can be cute, whereas the same child as an adolescent whose behaviour is difficult to manage can be extremely challenging for families. Older siblings can be resentful of the attention given to the child with special needs and create problems of their own, or they can be helpful and make a substantial contribution to the family's wellbeing. Younger siblings can create extra worries for parents, who often feel that they are unable to pay them sufficient attention.

Third, factors associated with the parents themselves and their relationship will have a major influence on family functioning. The parents' ages, personalities, financial status, employment status, educational levels and the state of their health will all affect the family. For example, older parents are likely to have fewer financial worries than younger ones, but may have more health problems of their own to worry about. Also, parents with extrovert personalities, who are optimistic and manage to keep a sense of humour, will typically experience less stress than those who tend to dwell on the negative aspects of the situation they find themselves in. In addition, a key factor in the functioning of the nuclear family is the quality of the parents' marriage. A healthy marital relationship will exert a positive influence on the family, whereas the consequences of an unhappy marriage are likely to be tension and conflict throughout the family microsystem.

Mesosystem
The family microsystem is influenced by the mesosystem in which it is embedded. The mesosystem comprises the range of settings in which the family actively participates, such as the extended family and the community in which the family lives. The extended family has a key role in determining how well parents cope with having a child with special needs. If extended family members, such as the child's grandparents, are understanding and supportive they can have a significant positive influence on family functioning; whereas if they are in conflict with the child's parents, or have little contact with them, the family misses out on an important source of support.

Neighbours, workmates, friends and other parents can also have a positive or negative influence on family functioning. When neighbours are friendly and allow the child with special needs into their homes to play with their own children, parents can feel pleased that their family is accepted in the neighbourhood. If neighbours are unfriendly then this can put an added strain onto the family. Workmates and managers can also have an influence on the family. For example, managers who are prepared to give parents time off work to attend important appointments concerning their children can reduce parents' stress levels and thereby contribute positively to family wellbeing. In contrast, workmates who talk of their own children's achievements while being too embarrassed to talk about the child with special needs turn a possible source of support into one of tension and unhappiness.

Typically, some of the parents' friends will find it difficult to adjust to them having a child with special needs and will tend to stay away. Parents themselves often shy away from many of their previous friends when they discover that their child has a serious illness or disability. This reduces the possible sources of support for the family. However, when parents meet up with other parents of children with similar difficulties they often form friendships which are very supportive and long-lasting. In many cases these friendships form an invaluable source of support for families.

The contacts which parents have with, for example, social workers, teachers and doctors can help to promote healthy family functioning if these professionals are sensitive, understanding, knowledgeable and supportive. Parents of children with special needs generally have a great deal of contact with professionals in the health, education and social welfare fields who can be an invaluable source of support and guidance; for example, regarding appropriate therapy, services and financial assistance. However, when parents find contacts with workers to be unhelpful, or even aversive, this increases stress and leads to reduced feelings of wellbeing within the family.

Exosystem
The mesosystem is itself influenced by the exosystem which consists of social settings which indirectly affect the family, such as the mass media, education system and voluntary agencies. First of all, the way children with special needs are portrayed in the newspapers or on television will have an impact on the family. For example, when stereotyped and patronizing attitudes towards people with disabilities are perpetuated by the media, this does not help families who have disabled members to integrate into the community.

Second, the quality and types of health, education and social welfare services available to parents will have a critical influence on the way in which these families cope with their child's special needs. This is made clear when families with disabled children in developing countries such as India are considered. In many cases of severe disability such children do not attend school, no financial assistance is available to parents and medical attention is inadequate at best. Families in this situation will clearly find life very difficult indeed. Although the picture in Western countries is generally much better, current political influences are forcing education, health and welfare services to operate like businesses. This is likely to have negative consequences for families of children with disabilities who typically need more intensive levels of help in these areas. For example, the availability of respite care for children with disabilities, so that families can have a break from time to time, is critical in helping many families cope. If the availability of this temporary care is reduced, then this will have a negative impact on the functioning of many families.

Third, the availability of various voluntary societies and support groups which have been established to help the parents of children with special needs can be a significant factor in determining how well these families cope. Many cities in the UK now have branches of the major voluntary societies such as MENCAP and a plethora of local support groups. For example, in Hull, which is a city of about 300,000 people, the local newspaper has a helplines column which lists support groups focused on a wide variety of special needs including autism, Down's syndrome, child abuse, cot death, mental illness, bereavement, and stepfamilies.

Fourth, the availability of recreation facilities, in the local community suitable for the participation of children with special needs, is very important in helping families cope. For example, institutions such as sports and leisure centres can ensure that they provide appropriate access and programmes for people with disabilities of various kinds. However, many parents find that recreational activities suitable for their children or young adults with disabilities in their local communities are inadequate, which results in these young people being bored at home for much of their free time and an additional strain being put on the family.

Fifth, the employment and residential opportunities available for adults who have a chronic illness or disability have an indirect effect on how families function. One of the most frequently mentioned concerns of parents who have children with special needs is anxiety about what will happen to their children in the future. In communities where there are various employment and residential options for young adults with such difficulties, parents' worries are minimized. When this is not the case an enormous strain is placed on parents in attempting to find suitable work and living arrangements for when their children leave school.

Macrosystem
Finally, there is the macrosystem, which refers to the attitudes, beliefs, values and ideologies inherent in the social institutions of a particular society, which all have an impact on the way a family of a child with special needs will function. First of all, the particular culture in which the family is living will have major effects on the family. If the culture is one which emphasizes humanitarian values, then there are much more likely to be positive attitudes towards people with chronic illness or disability than in cultures which emphasize materialism. Also, the specific type of society in which the family lives will have an impact on many different aspects of family life. For example, if the family lives in a rural community in a developing country then it may be easier to prepare a child with special needs for the types of work which are available than if the family lives in an urban community in an industrialized country.

The beliefs of the particular ethnic group to which the family belongs will exert an influence on the way the family reacts to the child's special needs. For example, there is a belief held by some people in traditional Samoan society that having a disabled child in the family is the result of the father being unfaithful to his wife, so that the child brings shame on the family. Religious beliefs also have a part to play in how families cope with having a disabled member. If the family believes the disabled child to be a gift of God, then it will be much easier for them to accept the situation than if the disability is seen as a form of punishment for some sin which has been committed. Another example is that in traditional Hindu families in India it is regarded as more important to visit the temple to make a gift to the relevant gods than to obtain therapy for the child.

The overall economic situation in the society in which the family lives will affect many aspects of how the family copes with having a child with special needs. Typically, in developing countries, where there is insufficient money available to provide essential health and education services to the community, many of the facilities which are available for children with special needs have been established by charitable organizations and a large proportion of such children do not receive appropriate health care, therapy or education. The professional guidance and financial support which are available to families in developed countries will also be mainly lacking in developing countries, which adds to the difficulties experienced by these families.

In countries which are better off economically, political policies will be instrumental in determining how the resources are distributed. When economic policies are more concerned with increasing profits than with improving the quality of life of the citizens, families who have members with special needs are likely to do less well. The political system in each country is responsible for the legislation regarding the rights of children with special needs and their families. The legal system has a role to play in interpreting the law in terms of individual cases of children with special needs. However, these cases typically indirectly affect large numbers of similar families since the legal rulings are often used to provide guidance for services in the health, education and social welfare fields. Recent years have witnessed increasing use of the legal systems in countries such as the USA and the UK, by parents attempting to ensure that their children with special needs receive the best possible services. The ability to engage in such a process is clearly important in determining the levels of support available to such families.

In conclusion, it must now be clear that how a family which has a member with special needs functions is influenced, not only by interactions within the family's microsystem, but also by its interactions with other levels of the entire social system, which all need to be taken into account by teachers when they are working with children with special needs and their families.

CHILDREN WITH DISABILITIES

Children with disabilities make up the largest group of children with special needs to be found in schools. The Warnock Report (DES, 1978) estimated that approximately one in six children would have special educational needs (SEN) throughout their school lives and one in five, or 20 per cent, would have such needs at some stage in their schooling. The largest proportion of children with SEN are those with mild learning difficulties who are sometimes referred to as slow learners, the vast majority of whom are educated in ordinary schools. Three other large groups of children with SEN are those with specific learning difficulties (dyslexia), moderate learning difficulties, and emotional or behavioural difficulties (EBD). Of these three groups the majority of children with EBD and specific learning difficulties are educated in ordinary schools. Children with moderate learning difficulties, most of whom used to be educated in special schools, are being integrated into mainstream schools in increasing numbers. Children with physical disabilities, hearing impairment and visual impairment make up only a small proportion of the population of pupils with SEN but are also being integrated into ordinary schools in increasing numbers. Therefore, teachers in mainstream schools are likely to have several pupils, possibly with different types of SEN, in their classes. Because of this, teachers need to be aware of the effects of children with disabilities on their families and to be able to work effectively with their parents.

Effects on families of children with disabilities

Mothers

Most of the research which has been conducted with parents of children with disabilities has focused on mothers and has shown that the bulk of the housework and child care in such families is carried out by them (Fewell and Vadasy, 1986). Despite the increased demands which a child with a disability makes on these aspects of family life, fathers generally do not make a bigger contribution than they make in ordinary families (McConachie, 1986). This may at least partially account for the fact that mothers of disabled children have been consistently found to have higher levels of stress and a higher incidence of stress-related physical and mental disorders than mothers of non-disabled children (Minnes, 1988). Mothers tend to be the ones who take children to their various appointments and have more contact with professionals, so have more opportunities to discuss their child's disability with them than fathers. Mothers also tend to have more contact with sources of support such as other mothers of children with similar disabilities, friends and family members. These factors are likely to help mothers to move through the adaptation process, which may lead to fathers experiencing greater difficulties than mothers in coming to terms with their children's disability.

Fathers
Since most fathers go off to work during the day and generally have other interests outside the home, their mental health may be less threatened than that of mothers by having a child with a disability. However, it is suggested that some fathers use denial in order to avoid facing up to the full extent of the disability or to hide their true feelings about the situation. In fact, the overall impression gained from the literature about effects on fathers of parenting children with disabilities, is generally a negative one. For example, fathers are often reported to have difficulty in accepting their child's disability, particularly if it occurs in a son or if the child is severely handicapped (Lamb, 1983). Also, fathers are reported to experience a higher level of depression, personality difficulties and marital relationship problems than fathers of non-disabled children (Meyer, 1986a and b). However, a recent detailed analysis of the literature found that the negative comments about fathers were based on very little hard data (Hornby, 1994a). Also, a recent study conducted by the author found little evidence for these negative effects on fathers. The 100 fathers of children with Down's syndrome, who were interviewed and completed questionnaires, were found not to differ significantly from other fathers on the variables studied, such as stress, depression, personality factors and levels of marital satisfaction (Hornby, 1995a and b).

Marital relationships
Much has been written concerning the potential marital difficulties faced by parents of children with disabilities (e.g. Featherstone, 1981). These difficulties are considered to be related to the additional demands of caring for a child with a disability, and various other factors. For example, it is suggested that spouses may disagree about the child's care or treatment and have insufficient time to resolve their conflicts. Having to deal with several professionals may increase the strain on parents, particularly since it is usually the mother who meets the professionals, and who has to re-interpret these meetings for the father. Also, as suggested above, because of greater involvement with professionals, the child, and sources of support, mothers sometimes move through the adaptation process more quickly than fathers, creating another potential area for conflict. Difficulties in sexual relationships may result from a lack of privacy, fatigue, a sense of isolation on the part of each spouse, or the fear of producing another disabled child.

The prevalence of marriage breakdown in such families has been the subject of considerable research. Early studies reported finding increased marriage breakdown and low marital satisfaction (e.g. Gath, 1977; Tew *et al.*, 1974) but more recent studies have generally found average levels of marital satisfaction and breakdown (Gath and Gumley, 1984; Hornby, 1995b; Roesel and Lawlis, 1983). An important and consistent finding is that a stable and satisfying marriage appears to reduce the stress experienced by parents in coping with a disabled child (Minnes, 1988). Some writers have suggested that having a child with a disability in the family tends to strengthen strong marriages and weaken fragile ones (Brotherson *et al.*, 1986).

Family life
The social life of many families with disabled members is likely to be restricted in one way or another (Lonsdale, 1978). Leisure activities such as participation in sports and other clubs, and family activities such as visiting friends, having picnics and attending family gatherings, are often affected. Many families are restricted in the use they can make of community facilities such as beaches, restaurants and public transport. There are also limitations in the type of holidays which families can take. The extent of the social restriction is greatest when the children are young, when physical handicap or behavioural problems are present, and when the degree of disability is severe (Gallagher *et al.*, 1983).

Families who have children with disabilities are also likely to have to meet additional expenses (Murphy, 1982). These are most often for medical care, clothing and transport. The family's income may also be reduced since one parent is prevented from going out to work because of the daily care requirements of the disabled child (McAndrew, 1976). Most developed countries have various financial benefits available to assist such families. However, surveys have shown that many parents do not receive the benefits to which they are entitled (Philip and Duckworth, 1982).

Siblings
Much has been written about the possible harmful effects on the siblings of children with disabilities, both by professionals (Seligman and Darling, 1989) and by parents themselves (Klein and Schleifer, 1993). It is suggested that there are several factors which can contribute to sibling maladjustment. Siblings may be given excessive caretaking responsibilities or may feel the need to overachieve to compensate for parental disappointment with the disabled child. Children may also wonder whether parents will expect them to care for their disabled sibling in later life and may worry about finding a spouse who would be willing to share such a responsibility. Other common concerns are anxiety about 'catching' the disability or about the future possibility of producing children with disabilities themselves (Simeonsson and McHale, 1981).

Siblings may feel isolated because their brother or sister is unable to share many of the experiences of growing up. This feeling is compounded by the family being somewhat cut off from the community because of the child with the disability. For example, siblings may feel embarrassed about their brother or sister and avoid bringing friends home, which may have a negative impact on their friendship network. Or they may feel resentment about the extra time and attention which parents give to their brother or sister with a disability. Siblings may feel guilty about their embarrassment or resentment or about feeling angry. They may also feel guilty simply because their brother or sister has a disability and they do not. Finally, such feelings are often compounded by the fact that siblings typically avoid seeking support from their parents since they feel that they have enough to cope with already (Powell and Ogle, 1992).

There are, however, several reports of the positive effects on sibling adjustment of having a disabled family member. One example of this is that many siblings are reported to choose careers in the helping professions such as teaching or social work (Crnic and Leconte, 1986). Other researchers have suggested that siblings of children with disabilities tend to be more insightful and tolerant of others' difficulties, to be more certain of their goals in life, to demonstrate greater social competence, and to develop a maturity beyond their years (Ferrari, 1984; Grossman, 1972).

Grandparents
A common source of support for the family may be the child's grandparents. Grandparents can provide emotional support, guidance about child care, access to community resources, as well as help with shopping, baby-sitting and financial support (Sonnek, 1986). However, some reports have suggested that many grandparents have difficulty adapting to the situation and either attempt to deny the reality of the disability or to reject the child (George, 1988). Another reported problem is the paternal grandmother's resentment of her daughter-in-law for not producing a normal child (Pieper, 1976). These difficulties can lead to a breakdown in the relationship between parents and grandparents, which is then likely to have a pervasive effect on family members. In fact, a recent survey of parents of children with severe learning difficulties found that there was a low level of support from grandparents (Hornby and Ashworth, 1994). A minority of grandparents provided a high level of support. More support was received from maternal grandparents than paternal grandparents. However, generally, grandparents were found to provide minimal support for families caring for their disabled grandchildren.

What teachers can do to help

It is clear from the foregoing discussion that a child with a disability affects all other family members to some extent, as well as having an impact on the parents' relationship with one another and family life in general. It is therefore important for teachers and other professionals who work with children with disabilities not to consider them in isolation but to take into account the entire family system of which they are a part, as elaborated below.

Consider whole family's needs
It is important for teachers to remember that any intervention they implement with a child with a disability will affect other members of the child's family, in particular the parents. So the impact of any intervention, such as a change of class or a home–school programme, on the wider family should be considered before it is implemented. In addition, the teacher needs to be concerned with the welfare of all family members and must be prepared to help parents deal with difficulties which they and other family members are experiencing that are related to caring for a child with a disability. For

example, parents should be informed about the support groups and work-shops (discussed in Chapter 6) which they, or other family members, would benefit from attending.

Maintain two-way communication
The most important way in which teachers can be of help to parents is for them to establish and maintain effective two-way communication between home and school. In this way any learning or behavioural difficulties which children experience can be dealt with quickly by teacher and parent working together. In addition, any other concerns which parents have about family members, or that teachers have about any aspects of the child's schooling, can be discussed openly and appropriate steps taken. Maintaining contact with parents by means of telephone calls, meetings and various written forms of communica-tion is discussed in detail in Chapter 3.

Sensitive communication of the results of assessments and reviews
Parents of children with disabilities often experience considerable anxiety about assessments and reviews of progress conducted with their children. They therefore need to be told assessment results, or be given a progress report, by a teacher who communicates empathy, sensitivity, openness, and a constructive outlook. Parents prefer to meet with teachers as soon as possible after an assessment is conducted, or a difficulty the child is having at school becomes apparent. Most parents prefer for both of them to attend such meetings and to have adequate time for asking questions.

Providing information
Parents need to have comprehensive, accurate and up-to-date information about the child's disability. Most parents also want suggestions about what they can do to facilitate the child's development. Many parents are interested in participating in some form of home–school intervention programme of the kind described in Chapter 4. Parents should also be informed about all the services and benefits available to help them care for their children. This infor-mation is widely available in the form of both written materials and profes-sional knowledge (Stone and Taylor, 1977). It is therefore quite alarming to discover how often it does not get to the people who need it. Teachers should therefore always check that parents have all the information they need about their child's disability and that they know about the relevant agencies and support groups which operate in their community. Making sure that parents know about the various grants and government benefits which they are eligible for is particularly important.

Providing support
Parents and other family members need to have supportive counselling avail-able to them from the diagnosis of disability onwards. In many cases this is provided by members of the extended family, or friends, or by other parents who have children with disabilities. But teachers also need to be able to

provide support. Parents are seldom willing to seek counselling for them-selves, whereas they will ask teachers about concerns they have about their children. This then provides an opportunity for teachers to use the listening and counselling skills which are described in Chapter 5, to deal with any other concerns parents may have and thereby facilitate their movement through the adaptation process, which was discussed earlier in this chapter.

Linking family members with others in similar circumstances
Most parents want to meet others who have children with similar disabilities. Although many parents wish to do this as soon as a disability is diagnosed, some do not want such meetings for several months or even years. When parents do meet others who have children with similar disabilities, they typi-cally gain substantial benefits both in terms of receiving emotional support and in obtaining information, such as about benefits available and respite care (Featherstone, 1981). Other family members, such as siblings and grandpar-ents, also gain greatly from meeting with their peers from other exceptional families (see Chapter 6). Teachers can help to facilitate these contacts by making families aware of the various support groups and other disability orga-nizations operating in their area.

CHILDREN WITH MEDICAL CONDITIONS

> Children with identified medical needs will not necessarily have an associated learning difficulty, but the consequences of their illness or condition may lead to future difficulties if there is not close collabora-tion between the school, the relevant child health services and parents. (DFE, 1994, p. 18)

This quotation from the *Code of Practice on Special Educational Needs* rein-forces the importance for teachers of considering the needs of children with various medical conditions. As suggested in the quotation, if appropriate help is not provided for such children, they are likely to develop learning difficul-ties or emotional and behavioural difficulties. It is therefore important to ensure that the special needs of these children are met so that such difficulties do not occur.

A wide variety of chronic and life-threatening illnesses are found among children in mainstream schools (Lansdown, 1980). The most common of these is probably asthma, with at least one in twenty children affected to some extent by this condition. Other common childhood diseases are eczema, diabetes, heart defects, epilepsy and rheumatoid arthritis. Medical conditions which are less common but which are often found in mainstream schools include cystic fibrosis, leukaemia, muscular dystrophy, kidney disease, aller-gies, haemophilia, sickle cell anaemia and phenylketonuria (PKU).

Teachers in mainstream schools are likely to have one or more pupils, with different medical conditions, in each of their classes. Therefore, teachers need to be aware of the effects of such illnesses on children themselves and on their families and to be able to collaborate with parents in meeting the children's special needs.

Effects on children of medical conditions

Children with chronic or life-threatening illnesses may have associated special needs for several reasons (Eiser, 1993). Children with conditions such as epilepsy or asthma may require drug treatment which can make them drowsy or impair their concentration. Children with life-threatening conditions such as heart disease, cancer, brain tumours or cystic fibrosis may need frequent hospital treatment. This necessitates them having considerable time off school which makes it difficult for them to maintain satisfactory progress. Also, the treatment required for some of these conditions involves chemotherapy or radiotherapy which typically leaves children feeling ill. Other chronic conditions such as eczema and rheumatoid arthritis may be painful and therefore deplete children's reserves of energy so that they cannot continue to work for long periods of time. They need more breaks in order to cope with fatigue. Finally, in dealing with children with serious illnesses, teachers may place more emphasis on social development and lower their academic expectations of children. Thus, all these medical conditions can have a negative impact on children's academic attainment.

In addition, suffering from a medical condition is likely to have a psychological impact on children. They may feel different from their peers and sometimes experience teasing or rejection because of their illness (Eiser, 1993). This can happen to children whose treatment has led to changes in their appearance, such as hair loss in the treatment of cancers. It can also happen to children whose illness prevents them from taking part in normal activities with their peers, such as for children with cystic fibrosis who need to spend most of their lunchtime receiving physiotherapy. Children may also have fears or anxieties about their illness which they are unable to express, or they may find it difficult to cope with the additional demands which their illness places on them, such as injecting themselves with insulin in the case of diabetics, or the restriction of their diet in PKU. Therefore, the psychological impact of such conditions can lead to children experiencing emotional or behavioural difficulties.

Effects of medical conditions on families

Children with chronic or life-threatening illnesses can be a major source of stress for their parents and other members of their families. Researchers have reported higher levels of stress and associated psychological problems in such families (e.g. Burton, 1974, 1975; Eiser, 1993). In many ways the effects on the family, including parents, siblings and grandparents, are similar to those found for children with disabilities, which were discussed earlier in this chapter. In general, the adaptation of family members to a child with a medical condition tends not to be related to the type or severity of the illness. Family adaptation is more clearly related to the social and emotional support available, parental health (both mental and physical), the quality of the marital relationship, and other family variables such as open communication, ability to express emotions, family cohesiveness, family stability, and the level of conflict within the family (Davis, 1993).

What teachers can do to help

The school has a very important part to play in the overall development of children who suffer chronic or life-threatening illnesses. Parents typically look to schools to provide a haven of normality for children whose lives are disrupted by their illnesses. Therefore, regardless of the severity of the illness, it is generally best to ensure that children's experience of school is as normal as possible. Eiser (1993) reports on research which suggests that the role of the teacher is vital in the successful integration of children with medical conditions into schools. In this regard, parents particularly appreciated several qualities in teachers. First, they valued teachers who exhibited a caring attitude towards their child. Second, they appreciated teachers who treated their child as normally as possible. Third, teachers who gave their children additional help with their work were rated highly. Fourth, they especially valued teachers who kept them well informed about what was happening in the classroom.

It is essential that parents, teachers and health-care professionals establish a working partnership in order to ensure that children's medical needs are met within an environment which is kept as normal as possible. To this end, Wadsworth *et al.* (1993) have suggested guidelines for teachers working with parents of children who have chronic or life-threatening illnesses. These are summarized below.

Establishing communication

Teachers need to establish effective two-way communication with parents in order to collaborate in resolving any difficulties which occur at school or at home. Parents should feel able to contact teachers about problems they are having at home. Likewise, teachers should feel able to seek parents' help in resolving any difficulties which occur at school. Strategies for achieving such two-way communication are discussed in Chapter 3.

Developing empathy

Teachers need to develop an understanding of the perspective of parents who have children with medical conditions and of the children themselves. It is important to take the time to develop rapport with the children and their parents. Teachers can help children to fit into class activities in ways which minimize the distractions caused by their medical needs. They need to be patient when dealing with parents' anxieties concerning their children and in encouraging parents to develop their children's independence and relationships outside the family.

Making home visits
Most parents appreciate teachers who are willing to make home visits in order to learn as much as possible about the child's medical condition. Home visits are also useful in developing rapport with parents who typically enjoy the opportunity of meeting with teachers in the more relaxed environment of their own home. Additionally, home visits enable teachers to assess home circumstances and observe children interacting with their parents. The information gained from these observations is often invaluable in planning to meet a child's special needs at school. Strategies for making successful home visits are discussed in Chapter 3.

Obtaining information from parents
Teachers need to ensure that they have obtained as much information as possible from parents about their children's medical conditions and related special needs. Information about children's medical needs is of primary importance, but it will also be useful to find out about children's likes and dislikes concerning such things as food and play activities. Finding out about any fears which children have and methods for managing their behaviour which are used at home will also be useful.

Liaison with health service personnel
Teachers need to liaise closely with health-care professionals responsible for the children in their classes with chronic or life-threatening illnesses. Effective communication between teachers, parents and medical personnel is clearly crucial in ensuring that the child's medical needs are met. Teachers may also need to be flexible in organizing classroom activities to take into account a child's medical requirements. They should be prepared to accept guidance or in-service training from health service personnel regarding such things as the administration of medication and the operation of special equipment. However, teachers cannot be expected to supervise extensive medical treatment at school. This must be the domain of qualified medical personnel.

Developing contingency plans
Teachers need to collaborate with parents in developing contingency plans for various situations which may arise. For example, what should the teacher do if the child becomes ill at school? What should the teacher do if essential equipment breaks down or if there is a power failure? Contingency plans for all such situations need to be written down and filed away ready for easy access by school staff.

Facilitating peer acceptance
Teachers will need to educate the rest of the child's class, and possibly other members of staff, about the child's medical condition. They can also facilitate peer acceptance of the child by such means as assigning the child 'buddies' or by using co-operative learning activities (Johnson and Johnson, 1987).

Designing Individual Education Plans

Teachers should ensure that parents and health-care personnel are fully involved in designing the child's Individual Education Plan (IEP), as well as in regular reviews of the child's progress. Strategies for facilitating parental involvement in the development of IEPs and reviews are discussed in Chapter 4. For a child with a serious medical condition it is also important to obtain appropriate participation of health-care professionals in the IEP and review processes.

Ensuring availability of support

Teachers need to ensure that parents are aware of the availability of sources of practical and emotional support for themselves and other family members. As discussed in Chapter 6, there is now a wide range of professional and voluntary agencies and groups offering support to families who have a child with special needs. An important function which teachers can fulfil for such parents is to find out whether parents have established a support network for their families and to alert parents to sources of support which they are not aware of. Teachers themselves are, of course, an important part of this network and therefore need to develop the listening and counselling skills discussed in Chapter 5.

Considering the entire class

Whereas parents' concern is understandably mainly for the welfare of their children, teachers must view the needs of the child who is ill within the context of the whole class. Meeting the special needs of such children cannot be allowed to jeopardize the education of other children in the class.

SUMMARY AND CONCLUSIONS

Teachers of children with special needs should be aware of the likely impact of caring for such children on members of their families. An understanding of the process by which parents and other family members come to terms with a child's illness or disability is therefore essential. Models for the adaptation process which have been discussed include ones which view it as comprising: stages of emotional reaction; a series of tasks or challenges; an examination of philosophical beliefs and values; and the re-experiencing of grief. Also essential is an understanding of the ways in which these families are affected by having a child with special needs. Family functioning is considered from the perspective of family systems theory and an ecological model which takes into account the influence of the social environment in which families live. It is proposed that if teachers are to establish productive working relationships with parents, then they need to have a comprehensive knowledge of the issues addressed in this chapter.

Chapter 8

Helping Parents of Children with Adjustment Problems

Two cases which were referred to me while I was working as an educational psychologist in New Zealand highlight the difficulties which teachers and parents have in coping with children with adjustment problems. The first was a 14-year-old boy who had been suspended from school for being disruptive and for using abusive language to a teacher. This kind of behaviour was uncharacteristic for this pupil so the school asked me, as their educational psychologist, to interview him and report to the governors on whether he should be reinstated or expelled. In the course of the interview it emerged that the boy's grandfather, whom he had been very close to, had recently died. He was clearly very upset and confused about this and had not had the chance to talk to anyone about it. When I passed on this information to the school governors they agreed to take him back and assigned a teacher he knew well to be available for him to talk to. His parents also said they would make sure that the family would help the boy to cope with his loss. Apparently, his uncharacteristic disruptive behaviour at school had been a cry for help.

The second case was of a 12-year-old girl who was referred to the psychological service in which I worked because she had been caught stealing both at school and at home. In the first interview it became clear that her stealing was also a cry for help. She lived with her father and step-mother, who, when I visited the home, was openly antagonistic towards her step-daughter. It also emerged that she was being prevented from seeing her natural mother with whom she still had a strong bond. I saw the girl for a few sessions of supportive counselling, during which time no further stealing occurred. However, I was unable to change her step-mother's attitude towards her and a few months later supported her decision to live with an aunt in a different district.

In my experience these cases are fairly typical of the way in which teachers and parents handle children's emotional problems resulting from their adjustment to a death or divorce in the family. Teachers react to the children's behaviour with disciplinary measures. Parents are not sure what to do, so they do nothing! When a death or divorce occurs it affects all members of the family. Parents may be struggling to cope with their own emotional adjustment and therefore may not be able to provide their children with the help that they need. Parents also may not be aware of their children's understanding of death or divorce or of the likely effects of such traumatic events on children. Most importantly, parents may not know what can be done to help children to cope. To make matters worse, children are often aware that their parents are upset following the death or divorce and tend to put on a brave face to avoid burdening parents further. So, because of this, and parents' preoccupation with their own pain, children's needs are often overlooked at home. This is why it is so important that teachers know how to help these children and are able to provide appropriate guidance to their parents.

This chapter considers the effects on children of bereavement and divorce, and provides guidelines for teachers in their work with parents whose families are experiencing either of these potentially traumatic situations.

CHILDREN COPING WITH BEREAVEMENT

A survey of 836 Year 7 students from six comprehensive schools in the north of England found that 61 per cent of them had experienced the death of a relative (Branwhite, 1994). Some children will lose a parent through death, while others will experience the death of a sibling or another close family member such as a grandparent. Others will have to cope with the loss of a close friend or someone they know less well such as a classmate or teacher.

It is clear that experiencing the death of someone close to them is a common occurrence among schoolchildren; however, it is one which is generally paid insufficient attention by parents and teachers. This is largely because most people know very little about children's reactions to death or how to help them cope with bereavement, so they tend to avoid the issue. The result of this is that many children have problems coming to terms with their losses.

The emotional and behavioural difficulties which are often experienced by children in coping with bereavement were first systematically studied by Rutter (1966) who found that twice as many children who had lost a parent by death attended the Maudsley Hospital psychiatric clinic than would be expected from death rates in the general population. He also found that about 14 per cent of children attending a child guidance clinic had been bereaved by the death of a close relative in the recent past. Rutter observed a variety of problems in children who had been bereaved, including anti-social behaviour, depression and various phobias.

More recently, Morgan (1985) has reviewed the literature on children's reactions to death and provides the following list of possible responses:

- regression to an earlier stage of development;
- hostile reactions to the deceased;
- hostile reactions to others;
- eating disorders;
- bedwetting;

- sleep disturbances;
- other psychosomatic disorders;
- attempting to replace the deceased;
- adopting the mannerisms of the deceased;
- aggressive behaviour;
- discipline problems;
- learning difficulties;
- denial;
- withdrawal;
- guilt;
- anxiety;
- panic.

Death of a parent

The death of a parent is generally thought to be the most traumatic event that can happen to a child. Morgan (1985) suggests that, when a parent dies, a child is faced with three major tasks. First, the child must come to terms with the reality of the death itself. Second, the child must adapt to the changes in the family which will result from the loss of a parent. Third, the child must learn to cope with the permanent absence of one parent.

Although guilt is probably an inevitable reaction to death for all ages, it can be particularly devastating to a child. Young children may believe that bad things happen because they have been naughty, so they may blame themselves for their parent's death. Children may react by regressing to an earlier stage of development or may attempt to deny the reality of the death by carrying on as normal and apparently being unaffected by it. But then children are likely to experience physical symptoms such as loss of appetite or sleep problems.

Children sometimes exhibit hostile reactions to their dead parent and other people, apparently because they feel they have been unjustly deserted by the deceased. Alternatively they may idealize the deceased as a means of avoiding the negative feelings they may have. Identifying with parents who have died by perhaps taking on some of their interests is seen as a constructive reaction, whereas trying to take their place, perhaps even developing some of the symptoms which appeared during the illness, is considered to be potentially harmful and should be discouraged.

The way in which children react to the death of a parent will be influenced by three factors (Morgan, 1985). One important factor is the age of the child, as discussed later in this section. For example, very young children and pre-adolescents may be the most vulnerable – very young children because they are still dealing with the issue of separation from their parents, and pre-adolescents because it is an important time for the development of sexual identity.

Another important factor is their relationship to the parent who has died. For young children the loss of the mother may have a bigger impact on them, particularly in traditional families where mothers spend considerably more time with the children than fathers. However, for boys who have reached school age, the death of their father may be more significant because of the loss of a male figure to identify with and to help in disciplining them. For example, it has been found that higher rates of delinquency are recorded for boys who have lost their fathers than those who have had their mothers die (Morgan, 1985). Also, when children are particularly close to one or other parent, as often happens, the loss of this parent will be more traumatic for them. In contrast, when children have a particularly strained relationship with one parent, the death of this parent can be accompanied by an improvement in their mental health.

Finally, a further factor in determining children's reactions to losing a parent is the extent to which previous losses and separations in their lives have been resolved. Children who are still coping with the death of someone close to them, such as a grandparent, may be particularly badly affected by the loss of a parent.

Morgan (1985) suggests that there are some common signs which teachers should look out for at school, that are indicative of children struggling to cope with the loss of a parent. These include: unsociability; despondence; forgetfulness; inattention; and a 'couldn't care less' attitude.

Death of a child

It is widely acknowledged that the death of a child is the most profound loss anyone can suffer and that parental grief is typically intense, debilitating and long lasting. Romanoff (1993) has suggested that six elements contribute to the severity of the loss. First, children carry with them many of parents' hopes and wishes for the future, so that when a child dies it is as if a part of the parent dies too. Second, particularly when an only child dies, loss of the parenting role can for many parents challenge their accepted meaning or purpose in life. Third, many parents have intense feelings of guilt about not preventing their child's death, no matter how irrational this may be. Also, because parents are struggling to cope with their own grief, they often find it difficult to adequately care for their surviving children and also feel guilty about this. Fourth, because the death of a child runs against the natural order of events, it challenges parents' fundamental assumptions about the universe and can leave them feeling vulnerable and afraid for the safety of other family members. Fifth, although parents tend to mourn their children as they existed at the time of death, they also mourn for their lost opportunities to experience developmental stages as the child's surviving peers reach them. Sixth, since childhood death is nowadays an infrequent event, there is often a lack of other bereaved parents to offer shared understanding and support. This is particularly important since the other sources of support typically used by parents, such as their spouse, friends and relatives, may be emotionally unavailable to them due to coping with their own grieving for the child.

Romanoff suggests that counselling can help parents in several ways. It can help to normalize parental experiences by educating them about what to expect. It can help parents to search for meaning in the death of their child –

something which is very difficult for parents to achieve by themselves. Counselling can also help parents to develop a re-defined purpose in life without the child by, for example, encouraging them in altruistic actions such as participating in support groups or starting a memorial fund. Finally, counselling can help parents find ways to continue their relationships with children who have died through inner representations while re-investing their energy in other relationships so that their lives can continue. For example, planting a tree or doing charitable work in the child's name or organizing a memorial service are ways in which parents can transform their relationship with their child who has died.

However, as noted earlier, very few parents avail themselves of counselling, which means that most parents are likely to be struggling to cope with their own grief for months or even years and therefore will be unable to provide sufficient help to their remaining children in coping with their reactions to the bereavement for possibly a substantial period of time. Morgan (1985) suggests that, when their own grief prevents parents from maintaining healthy parental relationships, surviving children are placed at risk of developing psychological problems. For example, younger children can react to the death of an older sibling by regressing to babyish behaviour in an attempt to prevent themselves growing to an age when death could occur. Alternatively, older children may become preoccupied with their own futures, anxious about whether they too will soon die.

Aware of their parents' grief, some children attempt to take the place of their dead sibling, perhaps by acting like them, even when this behaviour is not appropriate for their age. Children can experience considerable guilt, either about things done to, or not done for, dead siblings when they were alive, or about enjoying the feeling of having parents to themselves. If not recognized and dealt with during childhood, these guilt feelings can lead to depression which can carry on into adult life and in extreme cases become a precursor to suicide (Morgan, 1985). Another possible problem occurs when parents displace their negative emotions onto the remaining children. As parents attempt to adapt to their loss, the anger and other intense emotions they experience may be displaced onto the surviving children, who then sense their parents' hostility and feel that they are being punished for the death of their sibling.

Death of other significant people

It is often overlooked that the death of other family members such as grandparents, cousins, aunts or uncles can have a significant impact on children. This is especially so when there has been a particularly close relationship with the deceased. Also, the death of friends, classmates or teachers can be quite traumatic for children.

Incidents which involve the death of several schoolchildren, usually due to road accidents, tend to have a high profile because they are widely reported in the media. They actually happen quite infrequently but their impact when they do occur can be devastating to the families involved and to the children's school friends. The impact is of course greatest on those children who survived the accident, who commonly experience such reactions as depression, sleep disturbances, bedwetting, stomach problems, concentration difficulties and fear of hospitals, being hurt or dying (Morgan, 1985).

Unfortunately, the typical parental approach to children who have been affected by such an incident is to try to get them to forget the experience as quickly as possible. Parents not only avoid talking about it but also try to prevent children from discussing it with other people. Their reason for doing this appears to be a fear that children will become even more upset if they talk about it, whereas, by not discussing it openly, parents are adding to their children's trauma by indirectly suggesting that it is too frightening to deal with. In fact, parents are generally unaware that their unwillingness to discuss such things openly may have more to do with their anxiety about coping with their own reactions than about protecting their children.

The teacher's role

It is clear from the above discussion that a death in the family produces a situation for which parents need a great deal of help. Also, that the death of others with whom children have developed close relationships, such as friends, classmates and teachers, can be traumatic for children. Teachers are in the ideal position to provide help in coping with bereavement, both directly to the children concerned and indirectly through their parents (Thornton and Krajewski, 1993). First, teachers have a knowledge of child development and are therefore aware of the different levels of understanding of death which children have at different ages. Second, teachers are also experienced observers of children's behaviour and since they see children five days a week are in an excellent position to notice any behavioural changes which may indicate difficulties they are having in coping with a bereavement. Third, teachers have access to information on death and grieving either through Personal and Social Education curriculum material in their schools or through sources like those referenced in this section. Fourth, teachers will know of, or can find out about, the professional and voluntary help for the bereaved which is available in the local community. Finally, teachers provide a vital link between school and home. They can work closely with parents to ensure that children's needs are met.

However, although teachers are well placed to help children and their parents cope with bereavement, this frequently does not happen because death education has such a low profile in most schools. There has been a lack of training on the topic, so most teachers simply do not know enough about the grieving process and how to help children cope with it. Therefore, the following sections provide a summary of the knowledge teachers need to have in order to help children directly or to be able to provide guidance to parents so they can help their children to cope with bereavement.

What parents and teachers both need in order to be able to help children cope with bereavement is information about how children of different ages understand and react to death. They also need guidelines for helping children to adjust to their loss.

Children's understanding of death

Children's understanding of death progresses from a complete lack of awareness through several phases of increased comprehension until an adult view is attained (Morgan, 1985). From birth to approximately 2 years of age children are considered to have no concept of death as such. They may experience grief due to separation from people they have developed close relationships with, but have no realization of the finality of death.

Between the ages of 3 and 5, children tend to view death as being similar to sleep. They do not see it as a permanent state, nor do they understand that all living things must eventually die.

Between the ages of 5 and 9 years children come to realize the finality of death but still are not aware that it is universal. This usually happens from about 9 years of age, when children may become upset at the idea of death in general and in particular about the possibility of their parents dying.

From 9 to 12 years children become aware of the finality, inevitability and universality of death and because of this often experience some anxiety associated with such thoughts.

Teenagers tend to become defiant of death, almost daring death to occur by playing games such as 'chicken', in which they run across the road in front of cars.

Grief in children

Some writers consider that children go through similar stages of grief to adults, while other writers think that children's grieving is different, as suggested by the three-phase model proposed by Morgan (1985). The first phase is one of protest, when the child refuses to accept that the person is dead and, for some children, involves angry attempts to get them back. In the second phase children experience hurt, despair and disorganization as they begin to accept the fact that the person has really gone. The third phase is one in which hope develops as children begin to re-organize their lives without the deceased.

Worden (1991) suggests that there are several key points which people working with children who have been bereaved need to be aware of:

- experiencing the death of someone close is traumatic for children but need not lead to serious difficulties if appropriate help is given;
- how children mourn is determined by their levels of both cognitive and emotional development;
- children aged 5 to 7 years are a particularly vulnerable group since their cognitive development is such that they are beginning to understand the

finality of death but they do not have the personal and social skills to be able to cope with the situation;

- mourning a childhood loss can be re-triggered at various points during adult life, such as when the child gets married or reaches the same age as the parent who died;
- it is important for teachers and other professionals who work with children who have been bereaved to develop preventive approaches rather than waiting for problems to occur. In order to do this teachers need to understand the tasks involved in the process of mourning and to be familiar with the principles of grief counselling.

Grief counselling

Counselling must help the bereaved child to address the four tasks of mourning (Worden, 1991). These are:

1. to accept the reality of the loss;
2. to experience and work through the pain of grief;
3. to adjust to an environment in which the deceased is missing;
4. to withdraw emotional energy from the deceased and transfer it to other relationships.

According to Worden (1991) there are ten major principles and procedures of grief counselling. The application of these principles to children who have suffered a bereavement is discussed below.

1. Helping the child to actualize the loss
The first task of grieving is to fully accept that the loss has occurred – that the person is dead and will not return. This can be facilitated by encouraging children to talk about the person who has died and how the death happened. Family members and friends typically discourage children from talking about such things, either to spare their own pain or in the wrongly held belief that it is not helpful to dwell on the loss. However, like adults, children may need to talk about the death over and over again to someone who has the patience to listen. It may also be useful to suggest that children visit the grave of the deceased, or the place where their ashes have been scattered, and then encourage them to talk about their reactions.

2. Helping the child to identify and express feelings
Helping children to become aware of and express their feelings about their loss is the most important task of grief counselling. For younger children, drawing or painting can be used both to identify hidden feelings and as a trigger for getting them to talk about how they feel (Allan, 1988). For older children, getting them to write about the deceased can have a similar effect (Allan and Bertoia, 1992).

According to Worden (1991) the most problematic feelings experienced by people who have been bereaved are anger, guilt, sadness, anxiety and help-lessness. It is difficult for adults, let alone children, to realize that they feel anger towards the deceased. So this anger is generally projected onto other members of the family or doctors or other children or even teachers. Some-times the anger is turned inward and experienced as depression or guilt. Older children may feel guilty about how they behaved towards the deceased. Younger children may feel guilty because they believe that they were in some way responsible for the death.

Sadness is a natural reaction to a major loss, but the expression of sadness is often problematic. This is because it is best expressed through crying, which in some societies is discouraged since it is regarded as a sign of weakness. In other societies, such as among New Zealand Maoris and Jewish people, public crying is encouraged at funerals, which enables a healthy expression of sadness.

The anxiety experienced by bereaved children is partly related to their feelings of helplessness, of not being able to cope without the deceased parent or sibling. The anxiety also stems from children's increased awareness of the vulnerability of other family members and themselves to death.

3. Helping the child to live life without the deceased

As well as coping with their grief, bereaved children also need to be able to deal with the practical difficulties which result from their loss. A child who has lost a parent or an older sibling will probably be expected to take on more responsibility around the home. A child who has lost a close friend will need to seek out other friendships. Teachers helping children to adjust to these practi-cal difficulties need to use a problem-solving approach to counselling such as that described in Chapter 5.

4. Helping the child to re-invest emotional energy

Children need to be helped to find ways of maintaining the memory of the person who has died, while re-investing their energy in other relationships so that their lives can continue. For example, they can be encouraged to keep a journal of their thoughts about the deceased to help them see that by devel-oping new relationships they are not forgetting the person who has died.

5. Providing time to grieve

There is an expectation in most Western societies that people should 'get over' a major loss in a few months. In more traditional societies such as the Maori and Jewish cultures, referred to above, it is recognized that this is not the case. Both of these cultures have a memorial ceremony one year after the death to mark the end of the official period of mourning. Most experts in grief coun-selling agree that it generally takes up to two years for a child or an adult to adjust to any major loss. Also, that this only applies if people are grieving during this time and not avoiding expressing their feelings, in which case it may take much longer.

6. Providing ongoing support
Children will need continuing support for at least a year following the death, and probably longer. Certain times may be particularly difficult for them, such as birthdays, Christmas and the anniversary of the death. Bereavement support groups (discussed below) can be very helpful, so parents and children should be made aware of their existence in the local community.

7. Interpreting normal behaviour
Children can become frightened by their thoughts and feelings following the death of someone close. It is helpful to be able to explain the grieving process to them, including a discussion of typical reactions, in order to reassure them about the normality of what they are experiencing.

8. Allowing for individual differences
It is also important to explain to children that the reactions triggered by grief will be different for each person. Their surviving siblings, parents and friends will all be grieving in different ways.

9. Examining defences and coping style
Some of the ways in which children (and adults) cope with a bereavement are not healthy because they involve using defences to avoid experiencing the pain of grieving. For example, children who withdraw from contact with friends and family or refuse to talk about or look at photographs of the deceased are using defence mechanisms to avoid facing up to their grief and need help in order to develop more effective coping strategies.

10. Identifying pathology and referring
The listening and counselling skills discussed in Chapter 5 are sufficient for teachers to be able to help the majority of children to cope with bereavement. However, these will not be sufficient for a minority of children who are experiencing severe difficulties coping with their loss and who will therefore need more intensive help. Also, some teachers will feel that they do not have the expertise, time or patience to counsel children who have been bereaved. It is important to recognize one's limitations and be prepared to suggest to the headteacher or to parents that professional counselling is required.

Guidelines for working with children

Guidelines for teachers in working with bereaved children individually, or for class teaching about grief and bereavement, perhaps as part of the school's Personal and Social Education programme, are clear from the above discussion. The key points include:

- encouraging children to express feelings;
- discussing death in terms that children can understand;

- giving children information about death and grief suitable for their developmental level;
- suggesting appropriate ways in which children can remember the deceased;
- encouraging the adoption of healthy and effective coping strategies.

The way in which teachers react to and deal with death is vitally important since they act as models for their pupils. The impact on pupils of a school's approach to death is illustrated by the following quotation from a letter written by a mother whose 17-year-old son had recently drowned.

> I have two younger children, and their schools, with the best of intentions, told the other pupils not to mention the death in order not to upset them. Fortunately for my daughter, who was ten, a teacher at her school who had recently lost her husband realised that this was a mistake and countermanded these instructions. She told the other children that they should certainly talk to my daughter about her brother when she returned to school, at least to say how sorry they were. So my daughter was surrounded by loving, concerned friends, who talked to her quite openly about her brother ... My fourteen year old son was not so fortunate. His school mates obeyed the instructions ... he was deeply hurt by this apparent lack of concern: it seemed to him that the death was not important enough to mention. He was deprived of the support and care which his sister had enjoyed. (Mulder, 1994, p. 5)

Guidelines for working with parents

In addition to what teachers of bereaved children do at school they can be an invaluable support and resource for parents. Guidelines for teachers in working with parents of children who have been bereaved are outlined below.

Two-way communication
Keeping open channels of communication between school and home by such means as phone contacts, meetings and notes sent home (as discussed in Chapter 3) is the most important thing teachers can do to help parents. In this way concerns which either teachers or parents have about how children are coping can be shared and strategies for helping children can be agreed.

Providing guidance
Teachers can provide invaluable guidance to parents based on their knowledge of child development and of the effects of bereavement on children. Their knowledge of the children concerned and the working relationship they have established with the parents places them in an excellent position to provide this guidance. Teachers can recommend parents books about how to help children cope with their grief such as those by Dyregrov (1991) and Webb

(1993). They can also recommend books written for parents who have lost a child such as the powerful and moving book by Schiff (1977) and that by Rando (1988). In addition, they can suggest to parents books on death for surviving siblings to read (see Ordal, 1984).

Providing counselling
Teachers can provide supportive counselling to parents in order to help them cope with the effects of the loss on themselves and other family members. Mainly, what parents need is someone who can listen in order to help them clarify their thoughts and feelings and to help them to decide what to do about the various problems they face. The basic listening and counselling skills which teachers need in order to help parents in this way are discussed in Chapter 5. Most teachers do not have the time or skills to take on intensive or long-term counselling of parents, but even a brief session in which parents are encouraged to open up and are enabled to see the value of counselling can make them more likely to agree to being referred to sources of more specialized counselling and support.

Referring on parents to other sources of counselling and support
Teachers can help by making parents aware of the counselling services available in their community, particularly any which offer specialized help for people who have been bereaved. A very important source of support for parents and other members of families who have suffered a death are the bereavement groups which are now available in most communities. Such groups can help participants to gain hope, feel less isolated, develop feelings of fellowship, get information on other sources of help, and develop support networks (Hopmeyer and Werk, 1993). Often the most valuable things which people report gaining from participating in these groups are a feeling of not being alone in their grief and the opportunity to share thoughts and feelings with others who understand. Some groups are peer-led, others are co-led by a professional and a peer facilitator. They can be ongoing and open to new participants at any time or alternatively involve a pre-determined number of meetings, in which case they may be closed to new participants once they have begun. Whatever the organization, such groups can be an important source of support for the bereaved.

CHILDREN COPING WITH THEIR PARENTS' SEPARATION OR DIVORCE

Figures from the 1991 census show that, in Britain, one in three marriages end in divorce. Cox and Desforges (1987) report that, before they reach the age of 16, one in five children will experience the divorce of their parents, while an unknown number will be affected by parental separation. The survey of Year 7 pupils mentioned earlier in this chapter found that 25 per cent, or one in four pupils, had already experienced the separation or divorce of their parents (Branwhite, 1994). It has been estimated that around two-thirds of these children will exhibit noticeable changes in behaviour at school. The types of behaviour which are associated with parental separation and divorce include:

- restlessness;
- day-dreaming;
- withdrawal;
- concentration problems;
- aggressiveness;
- acting out;
- depression;
- regression to an earlier stage of development;
- loss of self-confidence;
- oversensitivity to criticism;
- peer relationship difficulties;
- deterioration in academic achievement;
- delinquency.

Children who experience the separation or divorce of their parents are therefore at risk of developing emotional and behavioural difficulties (Hodges, 1991). The likelihood that such difficulties will result depends partly on the extent to which their special needs are met within the school. In order for teachers to provide for the special needs of these children they need to know about the family difficulties which they are likely to experience and about the reactions to parental separation common to children of different ages. These aspects are discussed below.

Effects of separation and divorce on family members

Family disruption is often a serious problem in the first year after a separation. Parents tend to be so involved with their own feelings and concerns in adjusting to their new situation that they overlook the needs of their children. Discipline in the home can be inconsistent and parents may not notice the pain which children are experiencing. So at the very time when children need most support, their parents are least able to provide it because they are overwhelmed by their own problems. Studies of families where there has been a divorce, conducted in the USA (Morgan, 1985), have shown that at least one member of each family has exhibited disruptive behaviour or serious distress. In most cases the most seriously affected family members are the children. However, it must not be forgotten that parental divorce has an impact on all family members, including the extended family, especially grandparents, who face the possibility of being denied access to their grandchildren (Myers and Perrin, 1993).

Children's ability to cope with parental separation

A variety of factors contribute to a child's ability to cope with parental separation (Morgan, 1985). These are outlined below.

Age and gender of the child
In general, the older the child at the time of divorce the fewer detrimental effects there will be. However, there are differences in the ways children of different ages react to parental separation and these are discussed in the following section. Boys are generally considered to have more problems than girls in adjusting to divorce because typically it is the father who leaves the family home, depriving boys of a male figure with whom to identify.

Maturity of the child
How well children cope will depend on their emotional maturity and whether there are any other complicating issues in the child's life. For example, adopted children whose parents are divorcing tend to have greater difficulties coping with the situation than other children.

Financial situation of the parents
Often when one parent leaves the family home both parents face financial hardship. This may mean that custodial parents find it difficult to spare money for children to go on school trips or that non-custodial parents may not be able to afford to come to see children, or to take them out, as often as they would like.

Degree of discord before the divorce
For families in which there has been considerable conflict, hostility and instability, separation and subsequent divorce of the parents may be accompanied by feelings of relief in the children. Divorce may be easier for children in this situation to accept than those in families where parents have kept their disagreements away from the children.

Extent of conflict after the divorce
When both parents co-operate in maintaining relationships with their children following separation, it is much easier for children to adjust to the situation than when there is continual animosity between the parents. The most difficult situation for children to cope with is the one in which parents try to sour or break off the relationships between their children and the other parent. This situation almost inevitably leads to children experiencing emotional or behavioural difficulties.

Child's relationship with each parent
When a child is particularly close to the parent who moves out of the family home the separation will be much more difficult for the child to adjust to than when the child is closer to the parent who remains in the home.

Child's relationship with siblings
Children who have siblings typically find it easier to cope with divorce than only-children, since parental separation usually leads to siblings developing closer relationships with each other.

Child's own ability to cope with stress
Children will cope with the stress associated with parental separation in their own idiosyncratic ways. Exactly how they react will be influenced by their past experiences of coping with traumatic events.

Availability of emotional support
A major factor in determining how well children will cope with the divorce of their parents is the availability of people to talk to about their concerns and feelings. As suggested above, they may receive some support from their siblings, but other family members are likely to be too concerned with their own feelings to be able to help. This emphasizes the importance of children gaining support from people outside the family. Teachers are therefore key sources of support, since they typically know children better than any adult outside their families and can be confidential and objective in providing help.

Parental separation: effects on children at different ages

Pre-school-age children have difficulty fully understanding the situation and tend to react in one of two ways. They either attempt to deny the reality of the separation by pretending that nothing has changed or they become very upset and regress to more immature behaviour, with perhaps loss of independence in dressing, feeding or toileting. Pre-school children often fear the loss of the other parent when one has left the family home, so they may cling more closely to the remaining parent and tend to get very upset at routine separations (Cox and Desforges, 1987).

Children of primary school age tend to find it particularly difficult to adjust to parental separation since they understand enough about the situation to make denial a less useful option than with younger children, but at the same time they have not developed the coping strategies which older children typically use (Morgan, 1985). Common problems at this age are therefore associated with the feelings of guilt or anxiety which children may experience. They may feel guilty, believing that in some way they have caused the separation, or they may become anxious about the possibility of the other parent leaving them. Many younger primary school-age children experience feelings of intense sadness or depression which they find very difficult to understand. They can be highly emotional with aggressive behaviour alternating wildly with episodes of crying (Hodges, 1991).

Children of secondary school age tend to experience either anger or depression. Their academic work may be seriously affected or they may participate in delinquent acts (Morgan, 1985). They often experience embarrassment about the family break-up and try to keep it a secret from their friends.

They are much less likely than younger children to use denial or to regress in their behaviour. They have the ability to express their opinions and feelings, including their anger towards the parent they blame for the separation. Conflicts between both the parents and their teenage children may be intensified by the divorce.

What teachers can do to help

Teachers are in an excellent position to help children cope with the effects of divorce and to provide guidance to parents. First, teachers are knowledgeable about child development and are skilled in the observation and analysis of children's behaviour. They are therefore able to identify changes in children's behaviour which are indicative of their difficulties in adjusting to parental separation or divorce. Second, teachers are in regular contact with children and have the opportunity to develop sufficient rapport for them to feel comfortable enough to open up and talk about the things that are bothering them. Third, when teachers develop two-way communication with parents (as discussed in Chapter 3) they are in an ideal position to provide guidance to parents and to collaborate with them in dealing with children's difficulties.

Many children, whose parents have separated or divorced, report that they would have liked someone at the school to encourage them to talk about their feelings and reactions to their situation and suggested relevant books for them to read (Morgan, 1985). A range of specific strategies which teachers can employ to help children cope with the separation of their parents has been suggested by Cox and Desforges (1987). These are discussed below.

Developing a school policy
Teachers need to acquaint themselves with the school policy for dealing with the separation or divorce of parents of pupils attending the school. They need to know what is expected of teachers and of parents in the event of a separation. A school's expectations of parents in this situation should be written in the handbook which parents receive when their child enters the school. The statement needs to say that the school should be informed about any disruptions in home circumstances, including parental separation, which may affect a child's behaviour or progress at school.

Organizing support at school
For children who are experiencing disruption and unhappiness at home, the school can provide a haven of calm and security which itself is very therapeutic. In addition, having a well-organized system of pastoral care is very important so that pupils have the opportunity to develop a good rapport with their class teacher or form tutor, and head of year or head of house. Teachers acting in their pastoral capacity can thereby provide children with extra attention and support in order to help them cope with their parents' separation. Other members of the school staff, such as teacher aids and dinner ladies, can also provide such help, since pupils with difficulties often form a rapport with them.

Teachers can also ensure that the Personal and Social Education curriculum used in the school includes sessions on coping with parental separation and divorce. Alternatively, the topic can be made the subject of class discussions held during form tutor periods, using a developmental strategy such as that proposed by Allan and Nairne (1984) which uses an approach similar to that of the counselling model presented in Chapter 5.

Keeping records

It is helpful for teachers to keep records of the family circumstances of the pupils for whom they are responsible. Teachers need to have the names and addresses of both natural parents and any step-parents. They need to record when the separations and divorces have occurred and to have a record of the custody and access arrangements for each child whose parents have divorced. For example, is custody shared or does the child live mainly with one parent and see the other only at weekends? Teachers also need to record any legal restrictions placed on contacts between children and one or other of their parents. In addition, it is useful to keep a record of the problems which children have experienced at school since the separation. These records need to be continually updated and can eventually be made available to subsequent teachers.

Providing counselling

Teachers are in an excellent position to provide supportive counselling both to parents who have separated and to their children. Pupils are more likely to open up and talk about their problems with teachers or other school staff with whom they have developed a good rapport than with outside specialists such as educational psychologists or education welfare officers. The same applies to parents. They are much more likely to talk about their concerns to their children's teacher than to a professional counsellor. This is especially so when the teacher has established two-way communication with parents, as discussed in Chapter 3.

In order to provide supportive counselling to pupils and parents, teachers need to develop the listening and counselling skills discussed in Chapter 5. The model of counselling presented in Chapter 5 is one which is suitable for dealing with the vast majority of problems likely to be of concern to parents and children. However, the model emphasizes the importance of knowing when to refer parents or pupils for more specialist help. For example, while teachers may be happy to counsel parents about difficulties their children are having, it would be more appropriate to refer parents who want to discuss their own relationship problems to a specialist agency such as Relate.

Involving both parents

When teachers continue to involve both parents following a separation or divorce, it sends an important message to the children and their parents. This message is that children need both parents to be interested in their education and welfare despite the fact that they are now living apart. It is therefore important for teachers to send letters of invitation and copies of school reports to each of the parents. Divorced parents should be given the opportunity to decide whether they will attend parents' evenings together or separately. If they are able to attend together then the school can provide a neutral setting for parents to discuss their children's education. If necessary, teachers can act as child advocates, mediating on any conflict between parents.

Providing practical help
Teachers can provide help to divorced parents whose children live with them on a number of practical matters. First, since many families experience financial difficulties following a separation or divorce, teachers can check whether children are eligible for free school meals. Receiving free school meals not only eases the financial burden on parents but also communicates to other members of staff that parents may find it difficult to provide money for school trips and the like. Second, at times of family disruption children may not be able to find a calm place to do their homework, so the provision of a homework centre at the school can be a tremendous help. Third, practical considerations, such as providing a safe place for pupils to leave bags packed ready for weekend access visits, can make life easier for children and also reinforce the acceptability of their situation.

Providing relevant reading material
Teachers can help children adjust to their new situation by ensuring they have access to books which deal with separation and divorce, such as those by Mitchell (1982) and Townsend (1982). Teachers can also suggest books to parents which will help them to gain a better understanding of their children's needs following a separation, such as those by Burgoyne (1984) and Visher and Visher (1982).

SUMMARY AND CONCLUSIONS

This chapter has focused on how teachers can be of help to parents of children with two different types of special needs: children who have been bereaved and children whose parents have separated or divorced. Children's difficulties in coping with the death of a parent, a sibling or another person with whom they had a close relationship were considered. This section then focused on children's understanding of death at different ages and the principles of grief counselling applied to children. Then, guidelines for teachers in working with bereaved children and their parents were outlined. Also, the special needs of children whose parents have separated or divorced were discussed. The effects of parental separation on families were considered, specifically the factors associated with a child's ability to adjust to the new situation and the effects on children of different ages. Strategies which teachers can use to help the parents of these children were outlined, including developing a school policy and providing counselling.

In conclusion, it is clear that, in addition to providing appropriately for these children's special needs at school, teachers can be of invaluable assistance to their parents.

Chapter 9

Working with Challenging Parents

> Although the rewards are great, parent involvement presents numerous challenges to educators. (Karther and Lowden, 1997, p. 41)

Increasing the level of parental involvement in schools results in teachers interacting with more parents. Since parents, like teachers, have a range of personalities, some will be easy to work with and others will be more difficult. There will always be conflict caused by a small minority of parents. In fact, a certain amount of conflict has to be expected when parents and teachers work together, because they have different perspectives. Since parents are advocating for their own children it is impossible for them to be totally objective in their judgements. Sometimes their subjectivity leads to conflict with the teacher's views. Also, a general problem faced in education which does not apply in other professions is that, since everyone has been to school, just about everyone thinks they are an expert on education! The stance taken in this book is that, although parents should be viewed as experts on their children, teachers are the ones who should be regarded as experts on education. For these reasons, some conflict between parents and teachers is inevitable.

Therefore, although any expected difficulties are outweighed by the potential benefits, increasing the level of parent involvement will present significant challenges for teachers. There are two major implications of this. The first is that all types of parental involvement must be carefully set up so that, as far as possible, conflict between parents and teachers can be minimized. The second is that teachers must be aware of the types of difficulties they are likely to encounter, and need to know of appropriate techniques for dealing with them. They must also accept that, as Karther and Lowden (1997) suggest, 'Schools may be hard pressed to find methods that work with some parents' (p. 41).

During the final stages of writing this book I led a one-day workshop with a group of teachers in Barbados who taught children from pre-school to secondary level. After presenting some of the material from earlier in the book I asked them to brainstorm the various types of parents they found particularly difficult to work with. They came up with a list of seventeen different types, which are presented below in the order in which they emerged:

1. unsupportive parents;
2. hostile parents;
3. irresponsible parents;
4. abusing parents (physically, sexually, emotionally, neglectfully);
5. parents who have learning difficulties themselves;
6. poor or unemployed parents;
7. substance-abusing parents;
8. parents who are too busy;
9. parents who expect too much;
10. parents who expect too little;
11. parents with health problems;
12. threatening parents;
13. complaining parents;
14. parents with personal, marital or family problems;
15. very young parents;
16. parents without support;
17. professional parents.

This list compares fairly closely with the list of twelve problem parents presented by Seligman (1979) which follows:

1. hostile parents;
2. unco-operative parents;
3. perfectionist parents;
4. professional parents;
5. dependent parents;
6. overly helpful parents;
7. overprotective parents;
8. neglectful parents;
9. troubled parents;
10. fighting parents;
11. retarded or disturbed parents;
12. involved–uninvolved parents.

Combining these two lists and adding one other which presents a particular challenge to teachers – that is, relating to parents from different cultural backgrounds – produces a list of eight major types of difficulties. The remainder of this chapter will focus on the eight types of parents who are difficult for teachers to work with. For each type the aspects of the parents' behaviour which are challenging are clarified, the possible explanations for these are discussed and suggestions are made about how teachers can best work with such parents.

UNSUPPORTIVE PARENTS

It is particularly annoying to teachers when parents do not support their efforts in carrying out activities which are designed to involve them, such as in not attending parent–teacher meetings or not supervising children's homework. It often appears to teachers that these parents just do not care enough about their children, but this is seldom the case.

Explanations

There is a host of reasons why some parents appear unsupportive. Some parents may be so overwhelmed by the demands of caring for their family that they have little time or energy left for involvement in their children's education. Difficulties with arranging transport or child-minding may limit the involvement of many parents. Others may not perceive teachers to be approachable or schools to be welcoming and therefore avoid all contact. Still others may be embarrassed to interact with teachers because of their own difficulties when they were at school, or they may be anxious about teachers pointing out their children's deficiencies.

Approaches

Teachers must make an effort to use good communication skills so that parents see them as approachable. They should also do everything they can to let parents know that they are welcome at school. Teachers must attempt to get to know unsupportive parents better and to discover the source of the parents' lack of involvement, perhaps by means of a home visit (see Chapter 3). Listening skills can be used to identify the problem and, whenever possible, counselling skills used in order to work towards a solution (see Chapter 5). It may well be that alternative forms of interaction need to be considered; for example, the teacher making occasional phone calls to parents, or notes sent home with children, instead of expecting parents to attend meetings at the school.

UNCO-OPERATIVE PARENTS

Some parents are not just unsupportive: they are downright unco-operative. For example, some professional parents can be condescending, excessively critical or make unreasonable demands of teachers. Other parents give the impression of being too busy to devote time to activities such as listening to their children read at home. In contrast, some parents are so keen to become involved in activities, such as doing voluntary work in the school, that they can become too helpful and overstep their responsibilities or threaten to take over.

Explanations

As noted earlier, parents exhibit a wide range of personalities so it is not surprising that some parents will find it difficult to collaborate with teachers. Also, the low status of the teaching profession in the eyes of many members of the public, as well as the tendency of most people to consider themselves experts on education, means that some parents are too quick to criticize teachers and schools.

Approaches

Dealing effectively with unco-operative parents requires teachers to use the assertion skills which were discussed in Chapter 5. They should use the basic elements of assertiveness, discussed in that chapter, in all interactions with unco-operative parents. That is, they should be physically and vocally assertive and be prepared to use assertion muscle levels when necessary. They should use the four-step process presented in Chapter 5 to respond to criticism, and the guidelines for refusing a request to deal with unreasonable demands. They can use the modified DESC script to give feedback to parents who are too busy to become involved or overstep their responsibilities in school.

HOSTILE, COMPLAINING, THREATENING PARENTS

Some of the most difficult situations teachers have to deal with are when parents complain about something they see as the teacher's responsibility. Even worse are situations in which parents become aggressive or threaten teachers.

Explanations

There are three major reasons why parents become hostile to teachers. First, they may have a genuine grievance with the teacher for which they are justifiably angry. Second, another aspect of their lives has upset them or made them angry and they are inappropriately displacing this onto the teacher. Third, they have personal difficulties in relating to people generally and therefore tend to be aggressive with just about everyone.

Approaches

Whatever the reason for parents' hostility, the approach teachers should take is basically the same. It is very important that they follow the guidelines for dealing with aggressive behaviour which are outlined in Chapter 5. The key point is not to argue with parents but to stay calm and actively listen to what they have to say. By listening carefully, teachers can ensure that parents will calm down and can also determine whether parents' complaints are justified or not. If they may be justified then the four-stage process for dealing with criticism can be used. If a real problem is identified then teachers can use the six-step model for problem-solving which is outlined in Chapter 5 or the five-step model proposed by Beckman (1996) which involves:

1. identifying the problem;
2. generating alternative solutions;
3. evaluating solutions;
4. selecting the best solution;
5. implementing and monitoring the chosen solution.

When parents' complaints are not justified it is important to assertively refute them, but this can only be done when parents are no longer being aggressive. A useful strategy is the six-step assertion process proposed by Bolton (1979) in which active listening and assertive statements are used in a planned sequence to ensure that teachers get their point across while parents remain calm. The sequence of steps is as follows, adapted from Bolton (1979) and Hornby (1994b):

1. actively listen until parent becomes calm;
2. state teacher's/school's case assertively;
3. use silence to give parent time to think;
4. actively listen to clarify parent's response and defuse any further hostility;
5. recycle the process, repeatedly if necessary, until the parent accepts the teacher's point;
6. agree a solution, perhaps using the problem-solving process referred to above.

ABUSING PARENTS

Probably the most difficult type of parents for teachers to deal with are parents suspected of abusing their children. However, it must be noted that the most frequently occurring form of abuse is neglect and that this is often related to parents' financial difficulties (Berger, 1991). Teachers can therefore play an important role in identifying suspected cases of neglect and involving agencies who can provide the necessary support and guidance to parents. Teachers also have a role to play in identifying other types of mistreatment by parents; that is, physical, sexual and emotional abuse.

Explanations

The majority of abusing parents were themselves abused as children, so in most cases the abusers are also victims. However, being the victim of abuse does not always lead parents into child abuse. There are three pre-conditions for abuse to occur: a parent with the potential to abuse; a child who is for some reason seen as being different; and the occurrence of a stressful event in the family (Berger, 1991).

Approaches

The key roles which teachers play in all types of abuse are: identifying potential cases of abuse; referring these on to the member of staff responsible for dealing with such cases; and providing a supportive and caring environment for these children within the school. Apart from mild cases of neglect such as children wearing inappropriate clothing or occasionally appearing hungry, which can be tactfully discussed with parents, all suspected cases of abuse should be immediately referred on to the school's specialist. Therefore, teachers need to know how to identify the signs of the different forms of abuse children are subjected to. The following guidelines are adapted from Berger (1991).

Neglect
Neglect occurs when parents fail to provide adequate care, supervision, food, clothing and protection. The child is often hungry, dressed inappropriately, left unsupervised outside school hours or has medical needs which are not attended to. Neglected children often appear tired or hungry. They may steal or beg for food. They may come to school very early or stay very late. They may report that no one is at home to look after them.

Emotional abuse
Emotional abuse occurs when parents fail to provide the nurturing environment which is required for healthy development. Parents may be excessively harsh and critical. Rather than give praise and encouragement they withhold love and acceptance. Emotionally abused children may exhibit antisocial or destructive behaviour. They may be withdrawn or aggressive and exhibit self-stimulatory behaviour such as rocking. They may become involved in substance abuse or delinquency.

Physical abuse
Children who are physically abused show evidence of non-accidental injuries, of which bruises are the most common. Other indications are burns, abrasions, bite marks, cuts and fractures. Physically abused children may complain of soreness, move uncomfortably, avoid being touched and wear inappropriate clothing to cover the evidence. They may be afraid to go home or run away from home.

Sexual abuse
Sexual abuse takes a variety of forms, from inappropriate touching through to sexual intercourse. Children who are sexually abused are often difficult to identify, so teachers should discuss any suspicions they have with the member of staff who has had additional training in this area. Possible indications are when children are uncomfortable when sitting or walking, or are reluctant to change for physical education. Children may act in a seductive manner, display precocious behaviour or demonstrate knowledge of sexual behaviour

beyond their years. They may appear withdrawn or depressed or exhibit disruptive behaviour. They may be reluctant to go home or attempt to run away from home. When children confide in the teacher any incident of sexual abuse, this information must be immediately passed on to the staff member responsible.

PARENTS WITH PERSONAL, MARITAL OR FAMILY PROBLEMS

Parents who are wrapped up in their own problems are a great concern to teachers because it is clear that they are unable to pay sufficient attention to their children's needs in general and to playing their part in their children's education in particular.

Explanations

As discussed in Chapter 8, parents who are coping with the effects of traumatic events, such as a death in the family or separation or divorce, often become so overwhelmed by their own problems that children's needs are overlooked. Other personal problems may have the same effect; for example, when parents abuse drugs or alcohol. Marital problems and other conflict within the family can also result in insufficient attention being paid to children.

Approaches

It is not the teacher's place to become involved in parents' personal, marital or family problems, but neither can they stand idly by while their pupils suffer. When teachers suspect that parents' problems are interfering in their children's education they need to raise their concerns, tactfully, with the parents. This should be done in a face-to-face meeting with the parents, preferably at school but during a home visit if necessary. Most parents will appreciate the teacher bringing this to their attention. Teachers will need to use the listening skills and counselling skills presented in Chapter 5 to help parents to understand the problem and begin to decide what they can do to improve the situation. Teachers who use the skills outlined in Chapter 5 will be able to conduct this initial interview successfully. Once the problem has been acknowledged, parents can be referred on to individuals and groups in the community who can provide the specialist personal, marital or family counselling that is needed.

VULNERABLE PARENTS

Some parents have other problems which limit their ability to be involved in their children's education. They are vulnerable themselves and therefore need help in ensuring that their children's needs are addressed.

Explanations

Parents with their own health problems may not have the energy to assist in their children's education. Those who are unemployed or poverty-stricken will be impeded by financial constraints from participating fully in parental involvement. Young parents, poorly educated parents, those with little support from friends or family, and those with learning difficulties themselves will find it difficult to keep up their responsibilities regarding their children's education. These are the parents who are in most need of the help which teachers can provide, but they most often don't get it because they tend not to come into schools.

Approaches

Teachers need to reach out to these parents. If it is not possible to get them to come to the school, then home visits will be necessary. Teachers can use the skills outlined in Chapter 5 to help parents identify their problems and seek solutions. They can refer parents to relevant agencies to obtain any further assistance they need.

In many cases these parents will need guidance regarding their children's development and behaviour which, because of their experience with children, teachers are well able to give. Many of these parents will also benefit from the kinds of parent education discussed in Chapter 6. In fact, Karther and Lowden (1997) suggest that 'Parents with lesser education and limited resources have the most to gain from effective parent involvement activities' (p. 43).

PARENTS WHO EXPECT TOO MUCH OR TOO LITTLE

A common concern for teachers is parents whose expectations of their children are too high or too low. Some parents are too perfectionist in their demands of their children's achievements. Other parents are overprotective of their children and expect too little. These two types of parents are illustrated by the stories of Grant and Stephen which begin Chapter 6.

Explanations

Parents who expect too much from their children are often ones who have achieved very well themselves in their education or in their jobs and who find it difficult to accept that their child does not have the ability to achieve at the same high level. This situation is accentuated when the child has a learning difficulty or other form of special need. The need for parents to pass through a process of adaptation in order to come to terms with the child's special needs was discussed in Chapter 7. Parents of children with special needs are sometimes guilty of the opposite position: they expect too little of the child or are overprotective so that unnecessary limitations are placed on what the child can achieve.

Approaches

Teachers need to address the issue of expectations with such parents. They need to deal with them tactfully but assertively. It is counter-productive to get into an argument with parents about whether a child is capable of more or less. Teachers should keep the focus on an objective evaluation of what the child has achieved so far and on realistic suggestions of what should be tackled next. The counselling and assertion skills outlined in Chapter 5 will be useful in this regard.

PARENTS FROM DIFFERENT CULTURAL BACKGROUNDS

Teachers often find it difficult working with parents who come from different cultural backgrounds to themselves, and lower levels of parental involvement are usually in evidence for these parents (Harry, 1992).

Explanations

Parents who are from minority ethnic or cultural groups generally find it more difficult to interact with their children's teachers. Language difficulties may play a part in this, as does parents' apprehension about relating to teachers who are mainly from the mainstream cultural group. There are often also value differences, as in many cultures collaboration between parents and teachers is not seen as something which is necessary or even desirable.

Approaches

Teachers need to learn more about the cultural norms and values of parents from different cultural groups so that they can work more effectively with them (see Harry, 1992; Simpson, 1996). They should be prepared to adapt their expectations and means of communication in order to optimize the involvement of these parents.

SUMMARY AND CONCLUSIONS

This chapter has focused on eight types of parents who present particular difficulties to teachers. For each type the aspects of the parents' behaviour which are challenging were clarified, the possible explanations for these were discussed and suggestions were made about how teachers can best work with such parents.

Chapter 10

Strategies for Improving Parental Involvement

... schools may need to reconsider conventional assumptions and practices in order to build bridges to families who do not readily respond to traditional parent–school activities. (Karther and Lowden, 1997, p. 41)

A frequent response in workshops I have led on improving parental involvement has been that past attempts to increase the involvement of parents in schools have not been successful. Enquiry into what has been tried usually reveals that these attempts have involved putting more effort into developing existing forms of parent–school contact. This approach seldom works, but it is understandable that it is used since it is typical of the way people attempt to bring about change in many aspects of their lives. It has been referred to as 'first order change' by Rosenthal and Sawyers (1996, p. 195) who propose that what is really needed is 'second order change'. This involves a more drastic alteration in assumptions about working with parents, as well as the implementation of different strategies for parent involvement. It requires a re-evaluation of the basis for parent involvement and a willingness to try new approaches. In order to bring about such change, more systemic (Fisch *et al.*, 1983) and ecological (Bronfenbrenner, 1979) perspectives of the situation need to be considered.

From a systemic perspective, in order to bring about change in the *status quo* of minimal parental involvement, a strategic intervention is needed to disturb the equilibrium. The intervention needs to be strategic in that it is designed to disturb the *status quo* and therefore needs to be something quite different from what has been tried before. For example, Karther and Lowden (1997) suggest that 'Events at the school will draw more families if they are of an informal tone; if food, child care, and, if necessary, transportation are provided; and if the students participate in some way for or with their parents' (p. 43).

Using some of these ideas, an event can be organized which is sure to bring in the majority of parents of children attending the school. If teachers make a special effort to get to know as many parents as possible at this event it could be the trigger which breaks the cycle of low levels of parent involvement. Systems theory suggests that this intervention will initiate change in the whole system of parent involvement which previously existed at the school. Parents will then be more open to participating in a whole range of other activities, including those described in the model for parent involvement proposed in Chapter 2. Teachers need to capitalize on this situation by ensuring that the types of involvement outlined in this model are available to parents.

From an ecological perspective, the main objective of this book, which is to help teachers improve parental involvement in schools, can only be realized if the social environment in which teachers work supports parental involvement in education. Various components at different levels in the education system all have a part to play in determining just how effectively parents are involved in the education of their children. Attention must therefore be paid to all components in the process of improving parent involvement. These operate at four levels of the education system: government; local education authority; school; and teacher. Action needs to be taken at each of these levels in order to bring about long-term improvements in parental involvement. This is illustrated in Figure 10.1.

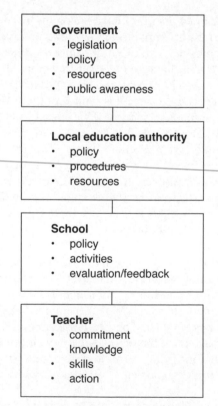

Figure 10.1: Strategies for improving parental involvement

GOVERNMENT

Legislation

The necessity for parental involvement in education needs to be enshrined in appropriate legislation like that in the UK and USA which is referred to in Chapter 1. Countries in which this is not the case need to make it a priority, since it is not possible to achieve high levels of parent involvement unless this is mandated by the laws of the land.

Policy

There needs to be a national policy on parental involvement in education which clearly sets out expectations for education authorities, schools, teachers and parents.

Resources

Governments need to provide sufficient finance to ensure that all components necessary to facilitate high levels of parental involvement can function efficiently. This includes money for both human and physical resources.

Public awareness

Governments need to disseminate the details of the existing legislation, policy in place and resources available to education authorities, schools, teachers and parents. This can be done through advertisements in the media, circulars to schools and education authorities, as well as leaflets for parents distributed through schools, libraries and health centres.

LOCAL EDUCATION AUTHORITY

Policy

Education authorities need to have a clear policy for parent involvement which draws on national policy and adapts this to local conditions and needs.

Procedures

Education authorities must have procedures in place for supporting schools in the implementation of their policy for parent involvement. They need to have officers who monitor what is happening in schools and offer support and advice to them.

Resources

Education authorities must commit sufficient resources to ensure the effective implementation of their policy and procedures. For example, many LEAs in the UK now have Parent Partnership schemes which are designed for this purpose. In addition, some schools have home–school liaison teachers whose function is to improve parental involvement at the school level.

SCHOOL

Policy

Each school needs to develop its own policy for parent involvement encompassing issues ranging from its philosophy on working with parents to the details of how parents are to contact teachers when they have a concern (for guidelines see Chapter 2). Also included must be the methods by which the details of this policy are communicated to parents and the roles of each member of school staff in implementing this policy.

Activities

Schools need to use a wide range of activities in order to achieve the greatest possible involvement of parents. These activities must address parents' needs and contributions at each level of the model for parent involvement presented in Chapter 2.

Evaluation/feedback

Schools should continually seek feedback from parents in order to evaluate the effectiveness of the parent involvement activities which they have in place. Schools should conduct regular needs assessments, survey current involvement of parents, and seek suggestions from parents about how their involvement can be made more effective (Rosenthal and Sawyers, 1996).

TEACHER

Commitment

Teachers need to be committed to working as closely as possible with parents. They need to embody the attitudes of objectivity, sensitivity, genuineness, respect, empathy and positive yet realistic thinking which were discussed in Chapter 1.

Knowledge

Teachers need to have an understanding of the typical problems which schoolchildren experience, as discussed in Chapters 7 and 8. They need to know about the wide range of strategies for parental involvement discussed in Chapters 3, 4 and 6. They also need knowledge of ways of coping with challenging parents, as discussed in Chapter 9.

Skills

Teachers need to develop the skills required for working effectively with parents which were outlined in Chapter 5.

Action

Teachers need to implement school policy and procedures for parental involvement. They need the courage and confidence to try out different ways of working with parents.

SUMMARY AND CONCLUSION

This chapter has made the case for using strategic interventions in order to initiate improvements in the level of parental involvement in schools. It also presented an ecological analysis of the key components involved in improving parental involvement, which focused on changes necessary at the levels of government, education authority, schools and teachers. Teachers have a key role to play in advocating for change at the levels of government and education authority, but their major responsibility is to bring about changes at the school level and in their own interactions with parents. It is hoped that the contents of this book will be helpful in these tasks and that teachers will feel empowered to take up the challenge of improving parental involvement in education.

References

Adler, A. (1927) *Understanding Human Nature*. Greenwich, CN: Fawcett.

Allan, J. (1988) *Inscapes of the Child's World: Jungian Counseling in Schools and Clinics*. Dallas, TX: Spring.

Allan, J. and Bertoia, J. (1992) *Written Paths to Healing: Education and Jungian Child Counseling*. Dallas, TX: Spring.

Allan, J. and Nairne, J. (1984) *Class Discussions for Teachers and Counsellors in the Elementary School*. Toronto: University of Toronto Press.

Atkeson, K. M. and Forehand, R. (1979) Home-based reinforcement programmes designed to modify classroom behaviour: A review and methodological evaluation. *Psychological Bulletin*, 86, 1298–1308.

Atkin, J., Bastiani, J. and Goode, J. (1988) *Listening to Parents: An Approach to the Improvement of Home–School Relations*. London: Croom Helm.

Attwood, T. (1978) The Croydon workshop for parents of preschool mentally handicapped children. *Child: Care, Health and Development*, 4, 79–97.

Attwood, T. (1979) The Croydon workshop for parents of severely handicapped school-age children. *Child: Care, Health and Development*, 5, 177–88.

Babcock, D. E. and Keepers, T. D. (1976) *Raising Kids O. K.* New York: Grove.

Ballantine, J. H. (1999) Getting involved in our children's education. *Childhood Education*, 75, 3, 170–1.

Bamford, J. and Arora, T. (1988) M. A. T. H. S. – Multiply attainments through home support: Progress and development. *Educational and Child Psychology*, 5 (4), 48–53.

Bastiani, J. (ed.) (1987) *Parents and Teachers 1: Perspectives on Home–School Relations*. Windsor: NFER-Nelson.

Bastiani, J. (ed.) (1988) *Parents and Teachers 2: From Policy to Practice*. Windsor: NFER-Nelson.

Bastiani, J. (1989) *Working with Parents: A Whole School Approach*. Windsor: NFER-Nelson.

Beckman, P. J. (1996) *Strategies for Working with Families of Young Children with Disabilities*. Baltimore: Paul H. Brookes.

Bell, R. Q. (1968) A reinterpretation of the direction of effects in studies of socialization. *Psychological Review*, 75 (2), 81–95.

Berger, E. H. (1991) *Parents as Partners in Education* (3rd edn). New York: Merrill.

Berger, M. and Foster, M. (1986) Applications of family therapy theory to research and interventions with families with mentally retarded children. In J. J. Gallagher and P. M. Vietze (eds) *Families of Handicapped Persons: Research, Programs and Policy Issues*. Baltimore: Paul H. Brookes, 251–60.

Berkowitz, B. P. and Graziano, A. M. (1972) Training parents as behavior therapists: A review. *Behavior Research and Therapy*, 10, 297–317.

Berne, E. (1964) *Games People Play*. New York: Grove.

Berrueta-Clement, J., Schweinhart, L., Barnett, W., Epstein, A. and Weikart, D. (1984) *Changed Lives; The Effects of the Perry Preschool Project on Youths Through Age 19*. Ypsilanti, MI: High Scope Press.

Bicknell, J. (1988) The psychopathology of handicap. In G. Horobin and D. May (eds) *Living with Mental Handicap: Transitions in the Lives of People with Mental Handicaps*. London: Jessica Kingsley, 22–37.

Blamires, M., Robertson, C. and Blamires, J. (1997) *Parent–Teacher Partnership*. London: David Fulton.

Bolton, R. (1979) *People Skills*. Englewood Cliffs, NJ: Prentice-Hall.

Bower, S. A. and Bower, G. H. (1976) *Asserting Yourself*. Reading, MA: Addison-Wesley.

Brammer, L. M. (1993) *The Helping Relationship* (5th edn). Boston: Allyn and Bacon.

Branwhite, T. (1994) Bullying and student distress: Beneath the tip of the iceberg. *Educational Psychology*, 14, 1, 59–71.

Broadfoot, P. (1989) *Reporting to Parents on Student Achievement: The UK Experience*. Working Paper No. 2/89, October, Bristol University.

Bronfenbrenner, U. (1976) Is early intervention effective? In A. M. Clarke and A. D. B. Clarke (eds) *Early Experience: Myth and Evidence*. London: Open Books, 247–56.

Bronfenbrenner, U. (1979) *The Ecology of Human Development*. Cambridge, MA: Harvard University Press.

Brotherson, M. J., Turnbull, A. P., Summers, J. A. and Turnbull, H. R. (1986) Fathers of disabled children. In B. E. Robinson and R. L. Barret (eds) *The Developing Father*. New York: Guilford, 193–217.

Brouillette, J., Thorburn, M. and Yamaguchi, K. (1993) Early childhood special education: An international perspective. In P. Mittler, R. Brouillette and D. Harris *Special Needs Education: World Yearbook of Education 1993*. London: Kogan Page, 175–84.

Bryans, T., Kidd, A. and Levey, M. (1985) The Kings Heath project. In K. Topping and S. Wolfendale (eds) *Parental Involvement in Children's Reading*. London: Croom Helm, 231–40.

Burgoyne, J. (1984) *Breaking Even: Divorce, Your Children and You*. Harmondsworth: Penguin.

Burton, L. (ed.) (1974) *The Care of the Child Facing Death*. London: Routledge and Kegan Paul.

Burton, L. (1975) *The Family Life of Sick Children*. London: Routledge and Kegan Paul.

Cattermole, J. and Robinson, N. (1985) Effective home/school communication – from the parents' perspective. *Phi Delta Kappan*, 67, 2, 48–50.

Chilman, C. S., Nunnally, E. W. and Cox, F. M. (eds) (1988) *Chronic Illness and Disability*. Newbury Park, CA: Sage.

Chinn, P. C., Winn, J. and Walters, R. H. (1978) *Two Way Talking with Parents of Special Children*. St Louis: C. V. Mosby.

Collins, D., Tank, M. and Basith, A. (1993) *Concise Guide to Customs of Minority Ethnic Religions*. Aldershot: Ashgate.

Corey, G. (1990) *Theory and Practice of Group Counseling* (3rd edn). Pacific Grove, CA: Brooks/Cole.

Cox, K. M. and Desforges, M. (1987) *Divorce and the School*. London: Methuen.

Crnic, K. A. and Leconte, J. M. (1986) Understanding sibling needs and influences. In R. R. Fewell and P. F. Vadasy (eds) *Families with Handicapped Children*. Austin, TX: PRO-ED, 75–98.

Cunningham, C. and Davis, H. (1985) *Working with Parents: Frameworks for Collaboration*. Milton Keynes: Open University Press.

Cunningham, C. C. and Jeffree, D. M. (1975) The organization and structure of workshops for parents of mentally handicapped children. *Bulletin of the British Psychological Society*, 28, 405–11.

Cyster, R., Clift, P. S. and Battle, S. (1979) *Parental Involvement in Primary Schools*. Windsor: NFER.

Davis, H. (1993) *Counselling Parents of Children with Chronic Illness or Disability*. Leicester: British Psychological Society.

DES (1967) *Children and their Primary Schools* (The Plowden Report). London: HMSO.

DES (1978) *Special Educational Needs* (The Warnock Report). London: HMSO.

DFE (1993) *Reports on Pupils' Achievements*. London: Department for Education.

DFE (1994) *Code of Practice on the Identification and Assessment of Special Educational Needs*. London: Department for Education.

Dinkmeyer, D. C. and McKay, G. D. (1976) *Systematic Training for Effective Parenting*. Circle Pines, Minn: American Guidance Service.

Dinkmeyer, D. C. and Muro, J. J. (1979) *Group Counselling: Theory and Practice* (2nd edn). Itasca, Ill: Peacock.

Dyregrov, A. (1991) *Grief in Children: A Handbook for Adults*. London: Jessica Kingsley.

Egan, G. (1982) *The Skilled Helper* (2nd edn). Monterey, CA: Brooks/Cole.

Eiser, C. (1993) *Growing up with a Chronic Disease: The Impact on Children and their Families*. London: Jessica Kingsley.

Elliott, J. A. and Hewison, J. (1994) Comprehension and interest in home reading. *British Journal of Educational Psychology*, 64, 203–20.

Epstein, J. (1985) Home and school connections in schools of the future: Implications of research on parent involvement. *Peabody Journal of Education*, 62 (2), 18–41.

Epstein, J. (1990) School and family connections: Theory, research and implications for integrating sociologies of education and family. In D. Unger and M. Sussman (eds) *Families in Community Settings: Interdisciplinary Perspectives*. New York: Haworth Press, 99–126.

Featherstone, H. (1981) *A Difference in the Family*. Harmondsworth: Penguin.

Ferrari, M. (1984) Chronic illness: psychosocial effects on siblings – I. Chronically ill boys. *Journal of Child Psychology and Psychiatry*, 25, 459–76.

Fewell, R. R. and Vadasy, P. F. (eds) (1986) *Families of Handicapped Children*. Austin, TX: Pro-Ed.

Fisch, R., Weakland, J. H and Segal, L. (1983) *The Tactics of Change*. San Francisco: Jossey-Bass.

Gallagher, J. J., Beckman, P. and Cross, A. H. (1983) Families of handicapped children: Sources of stress and its amelioration. *Exceptional Children*, 50, 10–19.

Gargiulo, R. M. (1985) *Working with Parents of Exceptional Children: A Guide for Professionals*. Boston: Houghton Mifflin.

Gath, A. (1977) The impact of an abnormal child upon the parents. *British Journal of Psychiatry*, 130, 405–10.

Gath, A. and Gumley, D. (1984) Down's syndrome and the family: follow-up of children first seen in infancy. *Developmental Medicine and Child Neurology*, 26, 500–8.

George, J. D. (1988) Therapeutic intervention for grandparents and extended family of children with developmental delays. *Mental Retardation*, 26 (6), 369–75.

Gitterman, A. and Shulman, L. (eds) (1986) *Mutual Aid Groups and the Life Cycle*. Itasca, Ill: Peacock.

Glynn, T. (1985) Remedial reading at home. In K. Topping and S. Wolfendale (eds) *Parental Involvement in Children's Reading*. London: Croom Helm, 181–8.

Glynn, T. and Glynn, V. (1986) Shared reading by Cambodian mothers and children learning English as a second language: Reciprocal gains. *The Exceptional Child*, 33 (3), 159–72.

Glynn, T., McNaughton, S. S., Robinson, V. and Quinn, M. (1979) *Remedial Reading at Home: Helping You to Help Your Child*. Wellington, NZ: New Zealand Council for Educational Research.

Gordon, T. (1970) *Parent Effectiveness Training*. New York: Wyden.

Graziano, A. M. and Diament, D. M. (1992) Parent behavioral training: An examination of the paradigm. *Behavior Modification*, 16 (1), 3–38.

Greening, N. and Spenceley, J. (1984) Paired Reading made easy. *Psychology*, 11 (2), 10–14.

Griffiths, A. and Hamilton, D. (1984) *Parent, Teacher, Child: Working Together in Children's Learning*. London: Methuen.

Grossman, F. (1972) *Brothers and Sisters of Retarded Children*. Syracuse, NY: Syracuse University Press.

Hannon, P. (1987) A study of the effects of parental involvement in the teaching of reading on children's reading test performance. *British Journal of Educational Psychology*, 57 (1), 56–72.

Hannon, P., Jackson, A. and Page, B. (1985) Implementation and take-up of a project to involve parents in the teaching of reading. In K. Topping and S. Wolfendale (eds) *Parental Involvement in Children's Reading*. London: Croom Helm, 54–64.

Harding, J. and Pike, G. (1988) *Parental Involvement in Secondary Schools*. London: ILEA Learning Resources Branch.

Harris, T. A. (1969) *I'm O. K. – You're O. K.* New York: Harper and Row.

Harry, B. (1992) *Cultural Diversity, Families and the Special Education System: Communication and Empowerment*. New York: Teachers College Press.

Henderson, A. (1987) *The Evidence Continues to Grow: Parent Involvement Improves Student Achievement*. Columbia, MD: National Committee for Citizens in Education.

Henderson, A. and Berla, N. (eds) (1994) *A New Generation of Evidence: The Family is Critical to Student Achievement*. Cambridge, MA: National Committee for Citizens in Education.

Hewison, J. (1985) Parental involvement and reading attainment: Implications of research in Dagenham and Haringey. In K. Topping and S. Wolfendale (eds) *Parental Involvement in Children's Reading*. London: Croom Helm, 42–53.

Hodges, W. F. (1991) *Interventions for Children of Divorce* (2nd edn). New York: Wiley.

Holland, S. and Ward, C. (1990) *Assertiveness: A Practical Approach*. Bicester: Winslow Press.

Hopmeyer, E. and Werk, A. (1993) A comparative study of four family bereavement groups. *Groupwork*, 6 (2), 107–21.

Hornby, G. (1980) Group counselling with parents of the intellectually handicapped. *Mental Handicap in New Zealand*, 5 (2), 3–14.

Hornby, G. (1982) Meeting the counselling and guidance needs of parents with intellectually handicapped children. *Mental Handicap in New Zealand*, 6, 8–27.

Hornby, G. (1987) Families with exceptional children. In D. R. Mitchell and N. N. Singh (eds) *Exceptional Children in New Zealand*. Palmerston North, NZ: Dunmore Press, 118–29.

Hornby, G. (1988) Launching Parent to Parent schemes. *British Journal of Special Education*, 15 (2), 77–8.

Hornby, G. (1989) A model for parent participation. *British Journal of Special Education*, 16 (4), 161–2.

Hornby, G. (1990) Training teachers to work with parents of children with special educational needs. *British Journal of In-Service Education*, 16 (2), 116–18.

Hornby, G. (1992) Group parent training using reflective counselling and behavioural training procedures. *British Journal of Mental Subnormality*, 38 (2), 79–86.

Hornby, G. (1994a) Effects of children with disabilities on fathers: A review and analysis of the literature. *International Journal of Disability, Development and Education*, 41 (3), 171–84.

Hornby, G. (1994b) *Counselling in Child Disability*. London: Chapman and Hall.

Hornby, G. (1995a) *Working with Parents of Children with Special Needs*. London: Cassell.

Hornby, G. (1995b) Fathers' views of the effects on families of children with Down syndrome. *Journal of Child and Family Studies*, 4 (1), 103–17.

Hornby, G. (1995c) Effects on fathers of children with Down syndrome. *Journal of Child and Family Studies*, 4 (2), 239–55.

Hornby, G. and Ashworth, T. (1994) Grandparent support for families who have children with disabilities: A survey of parents. *Journal of Child and Family Studies*, 3, 3, 403–12.

Hornby, G. and Murray, R. (1983) Group programmes for parents of children with various handicaps. *Child: Care, Health and Development*, 9, 185–98.

Hornby, G., Murray, R. and Jones, R. (1987) Establishing a Parent to Parent service. *Child: Care, Health and Development*, 13, 277–88.

Hornby, G. and Peshawaria, R. P. (1991) Teaching counselling skills for working with parents of mentally handicapped children in a developing country. *International Journal of Special Education*, 6 (2), 231–6.

Hornby, G. and Singh, N. N. (1982) Reflective group counselling for parents of mentally retarded children. *British Journal of Mental Subnormality*, 28, 71–6.

Hornby, G. and Singh, N. N. (1983) Group training for parents of mentally retarded children. A review and methodological analysis. *Child: Care, Health and Development*, 9 (3), 199–213.

Hornby, G. and Singh, N. N. (1984) Behavioural group training with parents of mentally retarded children. *Journal of Mental Deficiency Research*, 28, 43–52.

Hughes, N. and Carpenter, B. (1991) Annual reviews: An active partnership. In R Ashdown, B. Carpenter and K. Bovair (eds) *The Curriculum Challenge*. London: Falmer Press, 209–22.

Johnson, D. W. and Johnson, R. T. (1987) *Learning Together and Alone* (2nd edn). Englewood Cliffs, NJ: Prentice-Hall.

Jowett, S., Baginsky, M. and MacNeil, M. M. (1991) *Building Bridges: Parental Involvement in Schools*. Windsor: NFER-Nelson.

Karther, D. E. and Lowden, F. Y. (1997) Fostering effective parent involvement. *Contemporary Education*, 69, 1, 41–4.

Kelley, M. L. (1990) *School–Home Notes: Promoting Children's Classroom Success*. New York: Guilford Press.

Klein, S. D. and Schleifer, M. J. (eds) (1993) *It Isn't Fair! Siblings of Children with Disabilities*. Westport, CT: Bergin and Garvey.

Kroth, R. L. (1985) *Communicating with Parents of Exceptional Children* (2nd edn). Denver: Love.

Lamb, M. E. (1983) Fathers of exceptional children. In M. Seligman (ed.) *The Family with a Handicapped Child*. New York: Grune and Stratton, 125–46.

Lansdown, R. (1980) *More than Sympathy: The Everyday Needs of Sick and Handicapped Children and their Families*. London: Tavistock.

Lombana, J. H. (1983) *Home–School Partnerships: Guidelines and Strategies for Educators*. New York: Grune and Stratton.

Lonsdale, G. (1978) Family life with a handicapped child: The parents speak. *Child: Care, Health and Development*, 4, 99–120.

McAndrew, I. (1976) Children with a handicap and their families. *Child: Care, Health and Development*, 2, 213–37.

McConachie, H. (1986) *Parents and Young Mentally Handicapped Children: A Review of Research Issues*. London: Croom Helm.

McConkey, R. (1985) *Working with Parents: A Practical Guide for Teachers and Therapists.* London: Croom Helm.

McNaughton, S. S., Glynn, T. and Robinson, V. (1987) *Pause, Prompt and Praise: Effective Tutoring for Remedial Reading* (Book and Videotape). Birmingham: Positive Products.

Manthei, M. (1981) *Positively Me: A Guide to Assertive Behaviour* (revised edn). Auckland, NZ: Methuen.

Max, L. (1985) Parents' views of provisions, services and research. In N. N. Singh and K. M. Wilton (eds) *Mental Retardation in New Zealand.* Christchurch, NZ: Whitcoulls, 250–62.

Merrett, F. (1988) Peer tutoring of reading using the 'Pause, Prompt and Praise' techniques. *Educational and Child Psychology,* 5 (4), 17–23.

Meyer, D. J. (1986a) Fathers of handicapped children. In R. R. Fewell and P. F. Vadasy (eds) *Families of Handicapped Children.* Austin, TX: PRO-ED, 35–73.

Meyer, D. J. (1986b) Fathers of children with mental handicaps. In M. E. Lamb (ed.) *The Father's Role: Applied Perspectives.* New York: Wiley, 227–54.

Meyer, D. J., Vadasy, P. F. and Fewell, R. R. (1985a) *Living with a Brother or Sister with Special Needs.* Seattle: University of Washington Press.

Meyer, D. J., Vadasy, P. F. and Fewell, R. R. (1985b) *Sibshops; A Handbook for Implementing Workshops for Siblings of Children with Special Needs.* Seattle: University of Washington Press.

Meyer, D. J., Vadasy, P. F., Fewell, R. R. and Schell, G. C. (1985) *A Handbook for the Fathers Program.* Seattle: University of Washington Press.

Mink, I. T. and Nihira, K. (1987) Direction of effects: Family life styles and behavior of TMR children. *American Journal of Mental Deficiency,* 92 (1), 57–64.

Minnes, P. M. (1988) Family stress associated with a developmentally handicapped child. In N. W. Bray (ed.) *International Review of Research in Mental Retardation,* 15. London: Academic Press, 195–226.

Mitchell, A. (1982) *When Parents Split Up: Divorce Explained to Young People.* Edinburgh: MacDonald.

Mitchell, D. R. (1985) Guidance needs and counselling of parents of persons with intellectual handicaps. In N. N. Singh and K. M. Wilton (eds) *Mental Retardation in New Zealand.* Whitcoulls, Christchurch, NZ, 136–56.

Mittler, P. (undated) Checklist of questions on home–school links. Unpublished manuscript. University of Manchester.

Morgan, A. (1993) Training responses to the changing role of parents. *Community Education Network,* 13 (6), 2–3.

Morgan, S. R. (1985) *Children in Crisis: A Team Approach in the Schools.* London: Taylor and Francis.

Moses, R., Kamii, M. Swap, S. and Howard, J. (1989) The algebra project: Organising in the spirit of Ella. *Harvard Educational Review,* 59 (4), 423–43.

Mulder, V. (1994) Words can make it better. *Times Educational Supplement* (Review Section), 25 March, p. 5.

Murphy, M. A. (1982) The family with a handicapped child: A review of the literature. *Developmental and Behavioral Pediatrics,* 3, 73–82.

Myers, J. E. and Perrin, N. (1993) Grandparents affected by parental divorce: A population at risk? *Journal of Counseling and Development,* 72 (1), 62–6.

Newsome, E. and Hipgrave, T. (1982) *Getting Through to Your Handicapped Child.* Cambridge: Cambridge University Press.

Olshansky, S. (1962) Chronic sorrow: A response to having a mentally defective child. *Social Casework,* 43, 190–3.

Ordal, C. C. (1984) Death as seen in books suitable for young children. *Omega: Journal of Death and Dying,* 14, 249–77.

Patterson, G. R. (1975) *Families: Applications of Social Learning to Family Life* (revised). Champaign, IL: Research Press.

Philip, M. and Duckworth, D. (1982) *Children with Disabilities and their Families: A Review of the Research.* Windsor: NFER-Nelson.

Pieper, E. (1976) Grandparents can help. *The Exceptional Parent,* April, 7–9.

Pilgrim, M. (1999) Parental involvement in spelling. Unpublished MEd dissertation, University of Hull.

Powell, T. H. and Ogle, P. A. (1992) *Brothers and Sisters: A Special Part of Exceptional Families* (2nd edn). Baltimore: Paul H. Brookes.

Pugh, G. and De'Ath, E. (1984) *The Needs of Parents: Practice and Policy in Parent Education.* London: Macmillan.

Rando, T. A. (1988) *How to Go On Living When Someone You Love Dies*. Boston, MA: Lexingham.

Rinn, R. C. and Markle, A. (1977) Parent Effectiveness Training: A review. *Psychological Reports*, 41, 95–109.

Roesel, R. and Lawlis, G. F. (1983) Divorce in families of genetically handicapped/mentally retarded individuals. *American Journal of Family Therapy*, 11 (1), 45–50.

Rogers, C. R. (1980) *A Way of Being*. Boston: Houghton Mifflin.

Romanoff, B. D. (1993) When a child dies: Special considerations for providing mental health counseling for bereaved parents. *Journal of Mental Health Counseling*, 15 (4), 384–93.

Roos, P. (1978) Parents of mentally retarded children: Misunderstood and mistreated. In H. R. Turnbull and A. P. Turnbull (eds) *Parents Speak Out*. Columbus, OH: Charles E. Merrill, 245–57.

Rose, S. D. (1977) *Group Therapy: A Behavioural Approach*. Englewood Cliffs, NJ: Prentice-Hall.

Rosenthal, D. M. and Sawyers, J. Y. (1996) Building successful home/school partnerships. *Childhood Education*, 72 (4), 194–200.

Rutter, M. (1966) *Children of Sick Parents*. London: Oxford University Press.

Schiff, H. S. (1977) *The Bereaved Parent*. New York: Crown.

Schilling, R. F. (1988) Helping families with developmentally disabled members. In C. S. Chilman, E. W. Nunally and F. M. Cox (eds) *Chronic Illness and Disability*. Newbury Park, CA: Sage, 171–92.

Scott, L. (1993) *Governors and Special Educational Needs*. London: Advisory Centre for Education.

Seligman, M. (1979) *Strategies for Helping Parents of Exceptional Children: A Guide for Teachers*. New York: Free Press.

Seligman, M. (1990) Group approaches for parents of children with disabilities. In M. Seligman and L. E. Marshak (eds) *Group Psychotherapy: Interventions with Special Populations*. Boston: Allyn and BACON.

Seligman, M. and Darling, R. B. (1989) *Ordinary Families: Special Children*. New York: Guilford.

Shearer, M. S. and Shearer, D. E. (1972) The Portage Project: A model for early childhood education. *Exceptional Children*, 39 (3), 210–17.

Sicley, D. (1993) Effective methods of communication: Practical interventions for classroom teachers. *Intervention in School and Clinic*, 29 (2), 105–8.

Simeonsson, R. J. and McHale, S. (1981) Review: Research on handicapped children: Sibling relationships. *Child: Care, Health and Development*, 7, 153–71.

Simpson, R. L. (1996) *Conferencing Parents of Exceptional Children* (3rd edn). Austin, TX: PRO-ED.

Sonnek, I. M. (1986) Grandparents and the extended family of handicapped children. In R. R. Fewell and P. F. Vadasy (eds) *Families of Handicapped Children*. Austin, TX: PRO-ED, 99–120.

Sonnenschien, P. (1984) Parents and professionals: An uneasy relationship. In M. L. Henninger and E. M. Nesselroad (eds) *Working with Parents of Handicapped Children: A Book of Readings for School Personnel* (129–39). Lanham, MD: University Press of America.

Statham, J., MacKinnon, D. and Cathcart, H. (1989) *The Education Fact File*. London: Hodder and Stoughton.

Stewart, J. C. (1986) *Counseling Parents of Exceptional Children* (2nd edn). Columbus, OH: Merrill.

Stone, J. and Taylor, F. (1977) *A Handbook for Parents with a Handicapped Child*. London: Arrow.

Stone, L. (1993) Inspecting special: A new approach. *Special*, September, 33–7.

Sullivan, M. (1988) *Parents and Schools*. Leamington Spa: Scholastic Publications.

Sussell, A., Carr, S. and Hartman, A. (1996) Families R Us: Building a parent/school partnership. *Teaching Exceptional Children*, 28 (4), 53–7.

Swap, S. M. (1993) *Developing Home–School Partnerships*. New York: Teachers College Press.

Tavormina, J. B. (1974) Basic models of parent counselling: A review. *Psychological Bulletin*, 8 (11), 827–35.

Tavormina, J. B. (1975) Relative effectiveness of behavioral and reflective group counseling with parents of mentally retarded children. *Journal of Consulting and Clinical Psychology*, 43, 22–31.

Tavormina, J. B., Hampson, R. B. and Luscomb, R. (1976) Participant evaluations of the effectiveness of their parent counselling groups. *Mental Retardation*, 14, 8–9.

Tew, B. J., Payne, E. H. and Lawrence, K. M. (1974) Must a family with a handicapped child be a handicapped family? *Developmental Medicine and Child Neurology*, 16, 95–8.

Thornton, C. and Krajewski, J. (1993) Death education for teachers. *Intervention in School and Clinic*, 29 (1), 31–5.

Tizard, B., Mortimore, J. and Burchell, B. (1981) *Involving Parents in Nursery and Infant Schools*. London: Grant McIntyre.

Tizard, J., Schofield, W. and Hewison, J. (1982) Collaboration between teachers and parents in assisting

162   *References*

children's reading. *British Journal of Educational Psychology*, 52 (1), 1–11.
Topping, K. (1985) Review and prospect. In K. Topping and S. Wolfendale (eds) *Parental Involvement in Children's Reading*. London: Croom Helm, 287–96.
Topping, K. J. (1986) *Parents as Educators: Training Parents to Teach their Children*. London: Croom Helm.
Topping, K. (1995) *Paired Reading, Spelling and Writing: The Handbook for Teachers and Parents*. London: Cassell.
Topping, K. A. and Lindsay, G. A. (1992) Paired reading: A review of the literature. Research Papers in *Education*, 7 (3), 199–246.
Topping, K. and Wolfendale, S. (eds) (1985) *Parental Involvement in Children's Reading*. London: Croom Helm.
Townsend, S. (1982) *The Growing Pains of Adrian Mole*. London: Methuen.
Trotzer, J. P. (1977) *The Counselor and the Group: Integrating Theory, Training and Practice*. Monterey, CA: Brooks/Cole.
Turnbull, A. P. and Turnbull, H. R. (1986) *Families, Professionals and Exceptionality*. Columbus, OH: Merrill.
Vadasy, P. F., Fewell, R. R. and Meyer, D. J. (1986) Grandparents of children with special needs: Insights into their experiences and concerns. *Journal of the Division for Early Childhood*, 10 (1), 36–44.
Vadasy, P. F., Fewell, R. R., and Meyer, D. J. and Greenberg, M. T. (1985) Supporting fathers of handicapped young children: Preliminary findings of program effects. *Analysis and Intervention in Developmental Disabilities*, 5, 151–63.
Visher, E. and Visher, J. (1982) *How to Win as a Stepfamily*. Chicago: Contemporary Books.
Wadsworth, D. E., Knight, D. and Balser, V. (1993) Children who are medically fragile or technology dependent: Guidelines. *Intervention in School and Clinic*, 29 (2), 102–4.
Walker, C. E., Bonner, B. L. and Kaufman, K. L. (1988) *The Physically and Sexually Abused Child: Evaluation and Treatment*. New York: Pergamon.
Webb, N. B. (ed.) (1993) *Helping Bereaved Children: A Handbook for Practitioners*. New York: Guilford.
White, M. and Cameron, R. J. (eds) (1988) *Portage: Progress, Problems and Possibilities*. Windsor: NFER-Nelson.
Wikler, L. (1981) Chronic stresses in families of mentally retarded children. *Family Relations*, 30, 281–8.
Wikler, L. (1986) Periodic stresses of families of older mentally retarded children: An exploratory study. *American Journal of Mental Deficiency*, 90, 703–6.
Wikler, L., Wasow, M. and Hatfield, E. (1981) Chronic sorrow revisited. *American Journal of Orthopsychiatry*, 51, 63–70.
Williamson, D. L. (1982) *Group Power: How to Develop, Lead, and Help Groups Achieve Goals*. Englewood Cliffs, NJ: Prentice-Hall.
Wolfendale, S. (1983) *Parental Participation in the Education and Development of Children*. London: Gordon and Breach.
Wolfendale, S. (ed.) (1989) *Parental Involvement: Developing Networks between School, Home and Community*. London: Cassell.
Wolfendale, S. (1992) *Empowering Parents and Teachers*. London: Cassell.
Wolfendale, S. (ed.) (1993) *Assessing Special Educational Needs*. London: Cassell.
Worden, J. W. (1991) *Grief Counselling and Grief Therapy* (2nd edn). London: Routledge.
Yalom, I. D. (1985) *The Theory and Practice of Group Psychotherapy* (3rd edn). New York: Basic Books.
Young, S. J. (1991) The involvement of parents in the education of their physically disabled child. Unpublished MEd Thesis, University of Hull.

Name Index

Adler, A. 90
Allan, J. 80, 130, 139
Arora, T. 62
Ashworth, T. 116
Atkeson, K. M. 54
Atkin, J. 22, 24
Attwood, T. 92

Babcock, D. E. 91
Ballantine, J. H. 1, 2
Bamford, J. 62
Bastiani, J. 22, 25, 38, 41
Dattle, S. 22
Beckman, P. J. 146
Bell, R. Q. 106
Berger, E. H. 22, 107, 146, 147
Berkowitz, B. P. 55
Berla, N. 2
Berne, E. 91
Berrueta-Clement, J. 2, 51, 52
Bertoia, J. 130
Bicknell, J. 101
Blamires, J. 22
Blamires, M. 22
Bolton, R. 69, 74, 79, 146
Bower, G. H. 78
Bower, S. A. 78
Brammer, L. M. 69
Branwhite, T. 124, 134
Broadfoot, P. 64
Bronfenbrenner, U. 51, 107, 151
Brotherson, M. J. 114
Brouillette, J. 53
Bryans, T. 60
Burchell, B. 22
Burgoyne, J. 140
Burton, L. 119

Cameron, R. J. 26, 53
Carpenter, B. 66
Cattermole, J. 33
Chilman, C. S. 107
Chinn, P. C. 44
Clift, P. S. 22
Collins, D. 9
Corey, G. 88
Cox, K. M. 134, 137, 138
Crnic, K. A. 116
Cunnningham, C. 18, 19, 92
Cyster, R. 22

Darling, R. 115
Davis, H. 18, 19, 120
De'Ath, E. 22, 26
Desforges, M. 134, 137, 138
Diament, D. M. 55, 57, 91
Dinkmeyer, D. C. 86, 87, 90
Duckworth, D. 115
Dyregrov, A. 133

Egan, G. 80
Eiser, C. 119, 120
Elliott, J. A. 60
Epstein, J. 1, 4, 5

Featherstone, H. 25, 104, 114, 118
Ferrari, M. 116
Fewell, R. R. 113
Fisch, R. 151
Forehand, R. 54
Foster, M. 107

Gallagher, J. J. 115
Gargiulo, R. M. 22, 101
Gath, A. 114
George, J. D. 116

Gitterman, A. 95
Glynn, T. 50, 60
Glynn, V. 50
Gordon, T. 72, 73, 90
Graziano, A. M. 55, 57, 91
Greening, N. 60
Griffiths, A. 22
Grossman, F. 116
Gumley, D. 114

Hamilton, D. 22
Hannon, P. 58, 59
Harding, J. 22
Harris, T. A. 91
Harry, B. 150
Hatfield, E. 104
Henderson, A. 2
Hewison, J. 58, 60
Hipgrave, T. 57
Hodges, W. F. 135, 137
Holland, S. 75
Hopmeyer, E. 134
Hornby, G. 22, 27, 74, 80, 82, 86, 91, 92, 96, 101, 114, 116, 146
Hughes, N. 66

Jeffree, D. M. 92
Johnson, D. W. 121
Johnson, R. T. 121
Jowett, S. 22

Karther, D. E. 1, 142, 149, 151
Keepers, J. D. 91
Kelley, M. L. 54
Klein, S. D. 115
Krajewski, J. 128
Kroth, R. L. 22, 25, 38, 43, 42, 46, 76, 86

Subject Index